News Literacy

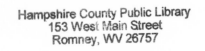

NEWS LITERACY

The Keys to Combating Fake News

Michelle Luhtala and
Jacquelyn Whiting

LIBRARIES
UNLIMITED™

An Imprint of ABC-CLIO, LLC

Santa Barbara, California • Denver, Colorado

Copyright © 2018 by Michelle Luhtala and Jacquelyn Whiting

Library of Congress Cataloging in Publication Control Number: 2018001665

ISBN: 978-1-4408-6152-9 (paperback)
　　　978-1-4408-6153-6 (ebook)

22 21 20 19 18 1 2 3 4 5

This book is also available as an eBook.

Libraries Unlimited
An Imprint of ABC-CLIO, LLC

ABC-CLIO, LLC
130 Cremona Drive, P.O. Box 1911
Santa Barbara, California 93116-1911
www.abc-clio.com

This book is printed on acid-free paper ∞

Manufactured in the United States of America

Contents

1

Introduction to News Literacy

The focus on fake news, "alternative facts," and general media mendacity distracts us from a very real educational challenge: teaching students the skills and dispositions that make them careful and thorough researchers. This is hard work, and there are no easy recipes to facilitate the process. However, with carefully scaffolded lessons that nurture students to become increasingly savvy inquirers, readers, and writers, librarians and content area educators can help students meet these challenges and become informed, active citizens. To that end, we will unpack the research that measures students' capacities for evaluating information, including the report by the Stanford History Education Group, "Evaluating Information: The Cornerstone of Civic Online Reasoning," and provide tiered lesson ideas and resources for educators to use with their students to teach them to be savvy in their consumption *and* creation of information. We believe that it is essential that students become skilled at critically examining the information they encounter in order to be valid creators of new information and participants in global discourse.

Fighting the digital media revolution—either personally or in our schools—is a quixotic endeavor. Students must learn to read for bias, shift between written and visually communicated information, and maintain focus amid a myriad of opportunities to depart from the primary text via hyperlinks to supplemental information. In fact, they and we are already engaged in these tasks, and educators should embrace the teaching of the skills necessary to read well in a digital environment rather than refusing to allow the digital world into their classrooms. To be critical consumers of the information they encounter, students need to learn to discern the connections among the array of topics and information presented in multimedia forms in order to make meaning of an information collection. Reading in a web-based rather than printed text environment requires students to develop information literacy skills specific to that medium, skills that go beyond traditional printed text literacy strategies.

It is important to draw a distinction between consulting a mainstream media news site for information and getting news updates from a social media feed.

The dissemination of click bait and intentionally misleading information that appears to be news largely happens via social media feeds. In May 2017, *Salon* provided this insight into web tools that are available to anyone doing searches or scanning news feeds in some popular social media:

Google's Fact Check. If your kid is researching information using Google News (either the site or the app), he or she may come across Google's Fact Check tag. A "fact check" only comes up if the story is controversial, which Google determines in various ways. Google doesn't label the story true or false, but it encourages users to do more digging.

Facebook's Disputed Tag. When stories have been flagged as iffy by users or Facebook's algorithm, Facebook checks with online fact-checkers Snopes and PolitiFact. If the stories are questionable, Facebook puts a "Disputed" note on them. Like Google, Facebook doesn't label the story true or false, but adding the Disputed tag should prompt kids to investigate further.

Twitter's Verified Accounts. Since so many people, including kids, get their news from Twitter, it's important to know whether tweets are legit or from a hacker, a fly-by-nighter, or another bad actor. Twitter's Verified Accounts add more stability and accountability in an effort to thwart false information, bullying, and audience manipulation. The company uses a thorough vetting process to determine whether a user is who they say they are and displays a blue check mark next to a verified user's name (Knorr).

To justify their expectation that students read only printed material, teachers anecdotally cite their concern that students' comprehension skills are eroding, as is their persistence with lengthy and complex texts, as though the tangibly printed words remove distraction and inherently invite engagement. Yet it does not make sense to resist the infiltration of the web into the classroom. We become less relevant if we do not embrace the teaching of information literacy (using information from any source) so that students develop into sophisticated consumers of digital and print media. In some ways, digital media further empowers the reader to control the reading process and experience. Web reading is (or can be):

- Nonlinear in its thinking requirements.
- Nonhierarchical in its organizational strategies.
- Nonsequential in its presentation.
- Multimedia (which requires significant visual literacy skills).
- Interactive so that readers control the pace and flow of the reading, not the writer, and can even offer comment on the substance of the writing.

Instead of becoming distraught about the possible adaptive changes to our brains as the means of reading evolves, we should be developing new pedagogy around literacy instruction to embrace these changes and maximize student potential. Graphicacy is a vital skill as more and more information is conveyed via sketches, diagrams, charts, and other forms of iconic representation or data visualization. The infographic is now mainstream in our lexicon and our content communication. Savvy readers evaluate nontext features like graphs and images. This isn't an innovation of the World Wide Web—there are charts and graphs and images in books—but the variation of the media and the volume of it in the media (since we're no longer constrained by pages and printing costs) are different and thus worthy of a new strategy. Students need to develop the ability to unpack and make meaning of the multimedia components in a digital text and synthesize the meaning they derive from each component.

These are sophisticated skills. They are high on Bloom's taxonomy. To dismiss the reading strategies necessary to understand the presentation of ideas in digital texts is to misunderstand or ignore the value of these texts—and their permanence. It is imperative that administrators and educators embrace the new media and invest in the professional development necessary to nurture students' literacy development in the digital age.

As veteran educators with 50 years' combined experience as both social studies educators and library media specialists, the authors, Michelle and Jacquelyn, bring to this issue and this pedagogy a wealth of resources and classroom-tested lessons that educators (librarians and their content area colleagues) can adopt, adapt, and implement. Collected and explained here is the model for research they can use, along with copious lessons that can be used with individual students or whole classes to reinforce and build information literacy skills at any point in their development.

REFERENCE

Knorr, Caroline. "Three Easy Ways Google, Facebook, and Twitter Help Kids Sniff out Fake News." *Salon*. Salon Media Group. May 12, 2017. Accessed January 2, 2017. https://www.salon.com/2017/05/12/three-easy-ways-google-facebook-and-twitter-help-kids-sniff-out-fake-news_partner.

2

A Brief History of Disinformation

The rise, in the 19th century, of William Hurst and Joseph Pulitzer to the ranks of media moguls gave these individuals and their publications control over the American public's access to information and redefined information literacy. The circulation wars that accompanied their rise in journalism eminence resulted in ever flashier, increasingly sensationalized headlines that captivated readers. When Hearst's *New York Journal* leveled unsubstantiated accusations at Spain for the sinking of the *U.S.S. Maine* in Havana Harbor, the U.S. public mobilized for the Spanish-American War, the first "media war" the United States fought. Congress may have declared the war and President William McKinley waged it, but the yellow journalism of the day fanned the fires of public opinion that sanctioned the intervention. Hearst and Pulitzer inaugurated what we now accept as status quo: the power of the media to influence public opinion. Their use of misleading, sensational headlines to sell newspapers in large part charted the course of U.S. diplomatic history.

Fast-forward to the 20th century, and satirical news broadcasts are main-stays of comedy programming. And the use of disinformation to manipulate people is ripe comedic fodder! In 2005, Stephen Colbert, on *The Colbert Report*, proclaimed that he would speak to America in plain English and coined the term "truthiness." Condemning reference material and books as elitist, Colbert lauded those who "know with their heart" rather than think with their head and pledged to feel the news at his audience. A season later, he again invoked truthiness when coining a new word: "wikiality," This term he derived from the premise that, if enough people agree with what you say, your assertion becomes truth. What is accomplished by this? "Bringing democracy to knowledge," Colbert would reply. The crazy person, Colbert intoned, is the one who goes against what the majority of people perceive to be reality. And as educators we know that groupthink, facilitated by crowd sourced information and like buttons, can undermine the development or the practice of critical thinking.

Stories have long been told with shades of truth—facts and depictions consciously manipulated to emphasize or highlight people or moments. When in

1817 artist John Trumbull was commissioned to create a painting commemorating the Declaration of Independence, he and the founders, including John Adams and Thomas Jefferson, in debating how to capture the historical importance of the creation of this document, decided that the signers of the document had to be depicted, along with opponents of the signing since their contributions were important to the final wording. Interestingly, signers who had already died and had not left behind a likeness from which Trumbull could work were omitted from the painting. The biggest irony to the truth of the painting is that the moment depicted didn't happen. Karie Diethorn, curator of Independence National Historical Park, explains the painting this way: "there's a romance associated with it and a belief that it had to happen that way—that these fifty-six men, like a chemistry experiment, were the catalyst that created America—poof" (Klein). So Trumbull, with the sanction of Adams and Jefferson, created a memory for us. One that is included in history textbooks across the country. One that informs our patriotic vigor. One that never actually happened.

Entertainment films display the disclaimer that they are based on a true story (which is different than actually being a true story). In 2012, film audiences were captivated by *Argo*, a Hollywood depiction of the rescue, in 1979, of potential American hostages when the U.S. embassy in Iran was overrun. The issue? To what extent was the role of the Canadian ambassador to Iran, Ken Taylor, and Canadian embassy staffer, John Sheardown, downplayed or ignored? In fact, the film became the subject of media examination in myriad publications, including *Slate* (Haglund). The choices made by the filmmakers in telling this story raise additional questions: Do the liberties taken in the making of this film matter beyond the insulting minimizing of the role of a friendly ally? And, most importantly, do audiences distinguish between documentaries and entertainment? Is being "based on a true story" true enough?

Long before the entertainment industry began playing with truth, we adopted into our lexicon "true facts," as though a fact was not, by definition, true. And, like Hearst and Pulitzer, other profit-seeking moguls have played with the dispersal of truth. "Snapple facts," which have adorned the underside of the ice tea bottle caps since 2002, persisted for a decade before their truthiness became suspect. *The Atlantic*, in 2013, published a review of Snapple facts by Adrienne LaFrance with the headline: "We Fact-Checked Snapple's 'Real Facts'; With 30 Seconds and a Web Connection, You Can, Too." His conclusions? "Some are true, some are outright false, and plenty others are incomplete or ambiguous to the point of absurdity. But it's easy to pluck out the spurious ones with a search engine and the right kind of bullshit detector" (LaFrance).

There it is.

We, the recipients of the truth, must accept it with a healthy dose of skepticism, the inquiry skills to examine it, and the willingness to disavow it even if we want it to be true. To that end, noted film director Werner Herzog said: "Facts do not convey truth. That's a mistake. Facts create norms, but truth creates illumination." Educators are in the business of nurturing illumination. Our charge is to help students build the skill repertoire necessary for savvy media consumption.

World leaders have long been aware of their ability and perhaps need to control the truth. And before there was Photoshop, magic could be worked with the art and science of photography in the darkroom. Robert Krulwich, in an episode of "Krulwich Wonders" on *RadioLab*, recounts the story one of his high school teachers told him about a photograph of Vladimir Lenin rallying troops about to be deployed to Poland. Leon Trotsky, a member of the Central Committee, was on the podium with Lenin that day, but he is missing from the official photograph. From the official photograph but not the original one. A few people were in line to succeed Lenin: Trotsky was one, and Josef Stalin was another. Lenin had Trotsky removed from the photograph to minimize his apparent importance to Soviet leadership (Krulwich). How's that for alternative facts? And from Russia, no less!

Truth seekers have emerged purporting to facilitate our separating fact from fiction in order to understand truth and make informed decisions as active citizens. Factcheck.org operates independent of any media outlet; their mission:

> We are a nonpartisan, nonprofit "consumer advocate" for voters that aims to reduce the level of deception and confusion in U.S. politics. We monitor the factual accuracy of what is said by major U.S. political players in the form of TV ads, debates, speeches, interviews and news releases. Our goal is to apply the best practices of both journalism and scholarship, and to increase public knowledge and understanding.
>
> FactCheck.org is a project of the Annenberg Public Policy Center (APPC) of the University of Pennsylvania. The APPC was established by publisher and philanthropist Walter Annenberg to create a community of scholars within the University of Pennsylvania that would address public policy issues at the local, state and federal levels ("Our Mission").

Politifact, on the other hand, is tied to the press. It is run by the writers and editors of Florida-based *Tampa Bay Times*, a self-described independent newspaper ("The Politifact Staff"). This phenomenon of media outlets becoming the watchdogs of their peers coincides with another development made possible by the ease with which information is digitally published and distributed: fake news. No longer must a person be a wealthy tycoon to start a media outlet. With a cell phone or computer and less than $100 for a domain name and hosting package, anyone—literally anyone—can become a citizen journalist regardless of his or her training, ethics, or motives.

In this critical information environment, we must remember the librarian's role: to collect, preserve, organize, and disseminate (CPOD) information. While we continue to be called upon for these purposes, we propose that the role of the K–12 librarian is a little different. We are educators, after all. Thus, it is incumbent upon us to fuel inquiry, nurture empathy, promote curiosity, foster skepticism, and empower innovation, while also teaching students to be savvy consumers of the information they seek and receive. The tools change. Our instructional strategies change. But our learning objectives are constant, whether teaching news literacy, promoting independent reading, or leading a maker project.

REFERENCES

Colbert, Stephen. "The Word—Truthiness." *The Colbert Report* video, 2:40. Comedy Partners. October 17, 2005. http://cc.com/video-clips/63ite2/the-colbert -report-the-word---truthiness.

Colbert, Stephen. "The Word—Wikiality." *The Colbert Report* video, 4:10. Comedy Partners. July 31, 2006. http://cc.com/video-clips/z1aahs/the-colbert-report -the-word---wikiality.

Haglund, David. "How Accurate Is *Argo*?" *Slate*. October 12, 2012. http://slate.com /blogs/browbeat/2012/10/12/argo_true_story_the_facts_and_fiction_behind _the_ben_affleck_movie.html.

Klein, Gil. "What's Wrong with This Picture?" *Colonial Williamsburg Journal*. Winter 2001. http://history.org/foundation/journal/winter11/painting.cfm.

Krulwich, Robert. "Krulwich Wonders: Whose Fingers Are on the Victoria's Secret Model's Shoulder?" *RadioLab*. WNYC Studios. February 1, 2012. http://radiolab .org/story/184792-krulwich-wonders-whose-fingers-are-victorias-secret -models-shoulder/.

LaFrance, Adrienne. "We Fact-Checked Snapples 'Real Facts.'" *Atlantic*. The Atlantic Monthly Group. October 11, 2013. http://theatlantic.com/technology/archive /2013/10/we-fact-checked-snapples-real-facts/280512/.

"Our Mission," *FactCheck.org*. Annenberg Public Policy Center. Accessed May 18, 2017. https://factcheck.org/about/our-mission.

"The PolitiFact Staff," *Politifact. Tampa Bay Times*. Accessed May 18, 2017. http:// politifact.com/truth-o-meter/staff.

3

What the Research Says about Students' Media Literacy

Interest in fake news exploded during the 2016 presidential election campaign. Simultaneously, educators were issued an apolitical call to action by the Stanford History Education Group (SHEG). This group, which brought us the "Reading Like a Historian" curriculum, published its research that measured the capacity of learners, grade six through higher education, to evaluate information. The executive summary for the 2015–2016 study, "Evaluating Information: The Cornerstone of Civic Online reasoning," uses words such as "bleak" and describes researchers' reaction as "appalled" when describing students' level of ability to unpack sources of information and distinguish fake from real and fact from propaganda. The study's designers had to redraft a few of the research instrument's tasks because students so drastically underperformed in the pilot (Wineburg et al.). (See Figure 3.1.)

As a consequence of its findings, SHEG offered the following recommendations to educators of students at all grade levels:

- Students as early as elementary school must learn how to distinguish online ad content from news content (p. 10).
- Students should learn to question everything they read, hear, and see in the media. For media consumers, healthy skepticism is healthy (p. 17).
- Students should be taught how to consume news delivered through social media outlets (p. 23).

That last point was reinforced by the United Nations Educational, Scientific and Cultural Organization's first of Five Laws of Media and Information Literacy:

Information, communication, libraries, media, technology, the Internet as well as other forms of information providers are for use in critical civic engagement and

9

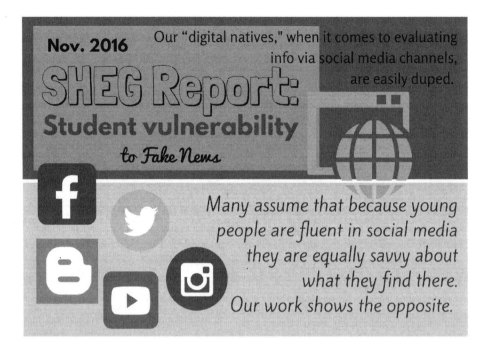

FIGURE 3.1   SHEG Report Infographic.

sustainable development. They are equal in stature and none is more relevant than the other or should be ever treated as such. United Nations)

The Internet has democratized information. News outlets, think tanks, and nonprofits are as likely (if not more so) to post their video stories and documentaries to YouTube channels as they are to host them on their own websites. We must question and accept the validity of information based on more critical and thorough examination than just its format.

This should be great news (no pun intended) to the 62 percent of Americans who, according to the Pew Research Center, get their news from social media sources (Gottfried and Shearer). It is possible to be both a social media junky and an informed citizen. Possible, but, without critical reading skills, is it likely? (See Figure 3.2.)

The list of people and organizations concerned about students' ability to make meaning of the flood of information they receive keeps growing. In February 2017, the Civic Engagement Research Group further validated the need to teach media literacy skills in K–12 education. Their study demonstrated that youth who described themselves as having media literacy training were more apt to detect misinformation than those who did not. The study concluded:

In short, the general concern for preparing youth to judge the accuracy of truth claims, such as the broader concern for the democratic purposes of schooling, should not be confined to a single priority such as media literacy. Rather, these

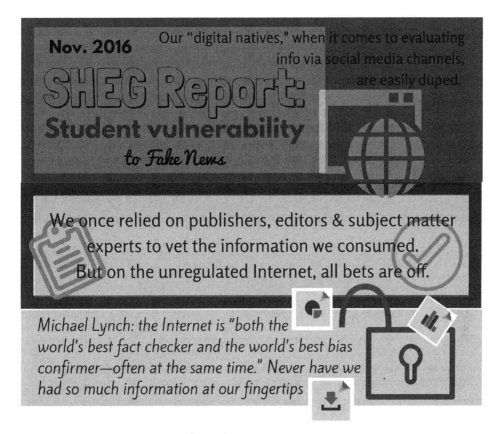

Nov. 2016   Our "digital natives," when it comes to evaluating info via social media channels, are easily duped.

SHEG Report:
Student vulnerability to Fake News

We once relied on publishers, editors & subject matter experts to vet the information we consumed. But on the unregulated Internet, all bets are off.

Michael Lynch: the Internet is "both the world's best fact checker and the world's best bias confirmer—often at the same time." Never have we had so much information at our fingertips

FIGURE 3.2   SHEG Report Infographic.

findings highlight dynamics worthy of study in multiple domains (Kahne and Bowyer).

In a March 27 *Washington Post* article about confusion among news consumers, Frank Sesno, a former CNN reporter and anchor who now runs George Washington University's School of Media and Public Affairs, was quoted as saying:

> One of the dangers is thinking that people know the difference between the editorial page and the front page, between a commentator or pundit commenting on something alongside a reporter who's supposed to be providing facts. In this environment, when you have news, talking points and opinions all colliding, it can be really disorienting to the audience (Farhi).

Add to that infotainment. How many people got their news from the likes of Stephen Colbert and Jon Stewart and now from Trevor Noah and John Oliver?

At all levels of the educational spectrum, educators have identified the need for increased critical thinking about sources of information. Before the SHEG report was released, before the 2016 election, University of Washington

Professors Carl T. Bergstrom and Jevin West began developing a one-credit course: "Calling Bullshit in the Age of Big Data." Their course title and expression of the course objectives might be pejorative, but they are valid.

> Our learning objectives are straightforward. After taking the course, you should be able to:
>
> - Remain vigilant for bullshit contaminating your information diet.
> - Recognize said bullshit whenever and wherever you encounter it.
> - Figure out for yourself precisely why a particular bit of bullshit is bullshit.
> - Provide a statistician or fellow scientist with a technical explanation of why a claim is bullshit.
> - Provide your crystals-and-homeopathy aunt or casually racist uncle with an accessible and persuasive explanation of why a claim is bullshit.
>
> We will be astonished if these skills do not turn out to be among the most useful and most broadly applicable of those that you acquire during the course of your college education (Bergstrom and West).

On their course website, you can find their lectures and other course resources, and you can follow them on social media for updates. (See Figure 3.3.)

Remember that fake news is nothing new, and that, in fact, our focus on it can lead us astray. If only fake news is being discussed when students are researching, then teachers and students are focusing on the wrong thing. Recognizing fake news doesn't even qualify for Band-Aid® status on the spectrum of media literacy challenges. Research is a process, and students often get through high school without learning it. They frequently approach research tasks knowing what they "want to say"—and then finding resources to support that. When they do this, they miss the point of research altogether, which is to:

- Explore a concept.
- Formulate a line of inquiry out of initial discoveries.
- Deepen knowledge by investigating multiple perspectives on the subject.
- Document developing learning.
- Synthesize learning into an original idea.
- Articulate and publish that idea.
- Incorporate new learning into their knowledge base for reflection and future retrieval and consultation.

These ideas are borne out by *New York Times* journalist Sarah Maslin Nir. During the "New York Times Learning Network" webinar on May 10, 2017, Nir remarked: "The way I see the world is the tip of the iceberg." This sentiment is true for us all; our challenge is to see the tip of the iceberg and then dive deep to see the whole thing! During the webinar, Nir went on to say that when we approach a story or research, we should "come with a thesis but hold it loosely." Remain open to possibilities. Finally, Nir described the process of researching

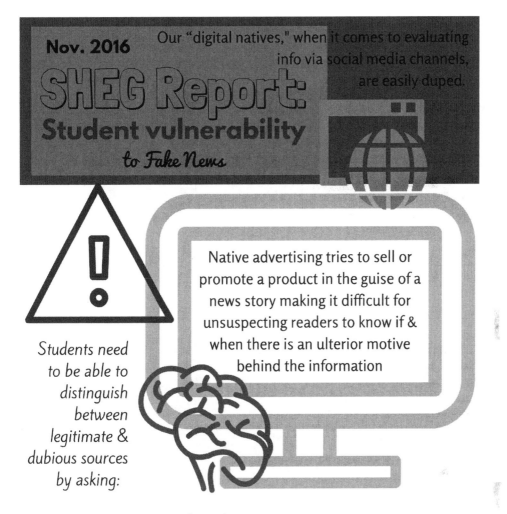

FIGURE 3.3   SHEG Report Infographic.

and writing her New York City nail salon expose, "The Price of Nice Nails." After initially being told that as a freelance journalist she didn't have the time for that kind of story, she renewed her request to investigate the plight of nail salon workers once she was hired as a full-time staffer. She initially took one month to research the story and present her findings to her editor. She was then told to take a year and continue working, which she did because, as she said, "you have to invest in truth." (See Figure 3.4.)

Nir's directive to journalists applies to news consumers as well. We all must invest in separating truth from fiction, information from persuasion, and reality from intentional deception. To be courageous, active citizens, students need to understand the role of the free press in a democratic society, as well as their role as news consumers. To do that, they must learn and remember these fundamental elements of media:

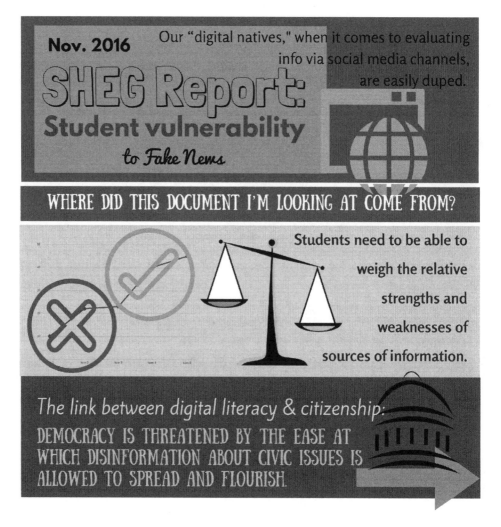

FIGURE 3.4   SHEG Report Infographic.

1. All media messages are constructed.
2. Media messages are constructed using a creative language with its own rules.
3. Different people experience the same message differently.
4. Media has embedded values and points of view.
5. Most media messages are organized to gain profit and/or power.

And in order to recognize these elements in the onslaught of media they engage with every day, they must internalize these questions in order to think critically about the information they encounter:

1. Who created this message?
2. What creative techniques are used to attract my attention?

3. How might other people understand this message differently from me?
4. What lifestyles, values, and points of view are represented in or omitted from this message?
5. Why is this message being sent?

There is a growing body of resources for this examination. Common Sense Media has long been a repository of tools and resources for developing media literacy and digital citizenship. In one of their articles about spotting fake news, they offered these general recommendations for students:

- Look for unusual URLs or site names, including those that end with ".co." These are often trying to appear like legitimate news sites, but they aren't.
- Look for signs of low quality, such as words in all caps, headlines with glaring grammatical errors, bold claims with no sources, and sensationalist images (women in bikinis are popular clickbait on fake news sites). These are clues that you should be skeptical of the source.
- Check a site's "About Us" section. Find out who supports the site or who is associated with it. If this information doesn't exist—and if the site requires that you register before you can learn anything about its backers—you have to wonder why they aren't being transparent.
- Check Snopes, Wikipedia, and Google before trusting or sharing news that seems too good (or bad) to be true.
- Consider whether other credible, mainstream news outlets are reporting the same news. If they're not, it doesn't mean it's not true, but it does mean you should dig deeper.
- Check your emotions. Clickbait and fake news strive for extreme reactions. If the news you're reading makes you really angry or super smug, it could be a sign that you're being played. Check multiple sources before trusting (Filucci).

The remaining chapters in this book explain the research process we use with our students and provide easy to replicate lesson ideas for each stage of the research process. The focus of these lessons is on developing students' critical reading and media literacy skills. Where possible, we have reproduced images, and frequently we direct you to create digital media snapshots because visual literacy is a key component of digital media literacy. In some cases, respect for intellectual property rights and copyright protections have prevented including images in this publication, although you are still able to replicate or project them for classroom use. We encourage you, in the context of your classrooms and libraries, to seek out these images for your students to examine.

REFERENCES

Bergstrom, Carl T., and Jevin West. "Syllabus." *Calling Bullshit: Data Reasoning in a Digital World*. University of Washington. Accessed May 18, 2017. http://callingbullshit.org/syllabus.html.

Farhi, Paul. "Sean Hannity Thinks Viewers Can Tell the Difference between News and Opinion. Hold on a Moment." *Washington Post*, March 28, 2017. http://washingtonpost.com/lifestyle/style/sean-hannity-thinks-viewers-can-tell-the-difference-between-news-and-opinion-hold-on-a-moment/2017/03/27/eb0c5870-1307-11e7-9e4f-09aa75d3ec57_story.html.

Filucci, Sarah. "How to Spot Fake News (and Teach Kids to Be Media-Savvy)." *Parenting, Media, and Everything in Between* (blog). CommonSense Media. March 20, 2017. http://commonsensemedia.org/blog/how-to-spot-fake-news-and-teach-kids-to-be-media-savvy.

Gottfried, Jeffery, and Elisa Shearer. "News Use across Social Media Platforms 2016." *Pew Research Center: Journalism & Media.* May 26, 2016. http://journalism.org/2016/05/26/news-use-across-social-media-platforms-2016.

Kahne, Joseph, and Benjamin Bowyer. "Educating for Democracy in a Partisan Age: Confronting the Challenges of Motivated Reasoning and Misinformation." *American Educational Research Journal* 54, no. 1 (February 2017): 3–34. http://civicsurvey.org/sites/default/files/publications/Educating_for_Democracy_in_a_Partisan_Age.pdf.

United Nations Educational, Scientific, and Cultural Organization. "Five Laws of Media and Information Literacy." *UNESCO Communication and Information.* Accessed January 3, 2018. http://unesco.org/new/en/communication-and-information/media-development/media-literacy/five-laws-of-mil.

Wineburg, Sam, Sarah McGrew, Joel Breakstone, and Teresa Ortega. *Evaluating Information: The Cornerstone of Civic Online Reasoning.* Stanford Digital Repository. 2016. http://purl.stanford.edu/fv751yt5934.

4

Echo Chambers, Filter Bubbles, and Likes, Oh My!

DO YOUR STUDENTS KNOW THERE IS A PROBLEM?

Students have learned what the "right" answers are when they are being asked about digital media and cyber conduct. But do they really understand why those answers are right? How many times have students shown you a website and told you that they know to look for a credible source, but this source has really good information for the topic of their research? It is clear by the "but" they are indicating that they know the source they are showing you is sketchy and somehow they want your permission to use it anyway.

When you ask students why they have to be careful about what they post online, do they tell you "because it is there permanently"? That is one of the right answers. But what happens when you ask those students how their postings are permanent or what it means to be permanent in cyberspace? Then what do they say? Probably that someone could screenshot their posts, so even if they are deleted another person has them. Most students don't push further and think about server farms and Internet archives or simply reposts.

Before you begin scaffolding lessons to address students' media literacy deficits, try some thought experiments. Ask students two questions. First, "Where do you get your news?" Have them collect their answers. Let them scroll through the apps on their phones or wherever they receive news feeds to compile their lists. Second, ask them, "When you learn about something important in the news, then where do you go? Why?" Have them do this in class. Choose a story from their feed that piques their interests and pursue it. This exercise asks students to confront their depth of understanding of any given issue. It also gives them an opportunity to reflect on whether they seek to confirm their bias or broaden their understanding.

17

Here is another experiment that helps to expose filter bubbles and the power of likes. Choose a single news source and set up a series of stations around your room. At each station, students will be able to access that source through a specific channel. For example, at Station 1 have a print copy of that day's *New York Times* (or some other widely distributed print publication). Station 2: the website edition of that publication. Station 3: the app for that source. Station 4: the individual student's Facebook feeds for that source. As students move through the stations, ask them to compare and contrast the different stories that appear and consider the connection between their social media likes and their feed.

Through these two exercises, you are helping your students to see that even if they are not filling the role of citizen journalist or creating and publishing digital content, they are participating in the curating of information. As participants in the process of information transmission, they have a civic obligation to critically consume the information they encounter and think before they like.

THE AGE OF THE CITIZEN JOURNALIST

This is a book about the meaning of, among other things, words so we must pause to consider this word: "citizen." Outside of national debates about the 14th Amendment, the word "citizen" has had special power when used in conjunction with titles or with other words that denote training or special qualifications. It can be a compliment or sign of respect to precede a title with the word "citizen."

> The U.S. president is a citizen commander in chief.
> George Washington is lauded as the Cincinnatus of his day for choosing the role of citizen over all others.
> We describe people as citizen scientists . . . or journalists.

Blogs allow ordinary people to have a voice, gain a following, and wield influence. "Blog" is both a noun and a verb. Both of the authors of this book blog. Some of the recommended resources in this book derive from blogs. Think about this word. When you regularly read the posts of a particular blogger, you are a follower. In 2002, the people of Baghdad began following the blog of a young man who wrote under the pseudonym Salam Pax as he documented the daily goings on in his city on the brink of war. In 2003, the reach of his blog exploded along with his country, and the government responded with random and sporadic censorship efforts.

Fast-forward to 2010 when demonstrations and uprisings rippled across North Africa and the Middle East in a movement called Arab Spring. Again, governments responded to the surging voices of the people by cracking down on Internet access and communication. People in these cities circumnavigated the obstacles by turning to social media to alert the world to the events that were happening around them. They live-tweeted and streamed video from cell phones to the world. People across the Arab world became citizen journalists.

In the midst of the Arab Spring revolutions, an Indian social activist, Anna Hazare, was waging a campaign against everyday corruption faced by people on a daily basis in India. Hazare, a 77-year-old man, was employing the traditional tactics of protest, including a hunger strike, and then chose to harness the power of the cell phone. When he asked his supporters to send him a text in support of his efforts, 80,000 people heeded his request. And that was just the beginning. In his TED Talk, "What New Power Looks Like," Jeremy Heimans explains that, in order to avoid the charges incurred by calling and texting, in some parts of the world it is common practice to leave a missed call. So Hazare asked his supporters to do just that—leave him a missed call, and 35 million people did. In Heimans's words: "So this is one of the largest coordinated actions in human history. It's remarkable."

So what has changed since Pax started blogging about his country's war in 2002? The mode of digital communication. You can subscribe to a blog, you can follow a blogger, but the content isn't culled for you. When the blogger posts, you receive the post in your feed. The post isn't tailored to your tastes, interests, or political proclivities in any way. But when you like something on social media, you are providing information about what you like and believe. And every time you like something, what you see—both content and advertisements—is curated to match your tastes. Yet we have the perception that social media connects us to the world and that it has democratized information. This may be true but only if we remain open to that which we dislike as much as that which we like. Where does Hazare come in? Like the citizen journalists of Arab Spring, all you need is a cell phone to mobilize millions of people.

And the lines between what is social, what is activism, and what is news continue to interweave and blur. Periscope allows for live streaming to Twitter, and Facebook live broadcasts are proliferating. "Real News" shows are being launched on Facebook. That makes teaching students the difference between news and opinion tricky, to say the least.

REFERENCE

Heimans, Jeremy. "What New Power Looks Like." TED video, 15:09. June 2014. Accessed January 3, 2017. https://www.ted.com/talks/jeremy_heimans_what_new_power_looks_like/transcript.

5

The Stages of Research: A Model

Research is a recursive process that culminates in the effective expression of an original idea informed by new learning that deepens in its complexity as learners move through the phases. An essential element of effective and purposeful instruction and collaboration with colleagues is focused on helping students learn the strategies and best practices for conducting research. School librarians are essential partners with classroom teachers when it comes to helping students focus their research topics, develop research questions, and collect lists of keywords for searching. Librarians also coach students to reflect as they find information and revise their questions and terms to reflect their learning. As students find, vet, and cite sources, the school librarian is a vital resource for supporting this work. Finally, in partnership with the classroom teacher, librarians provide instruction to guide students' note taking, thesis development, and the crafting of the final presentations of their learning.

A component of the role of the school librarian is as an advocate for the library program and the inclusion of information literacy skill practice in the curricula of various departments. When it comes to implementing research practice, there is obvious overlap with the curricula of the social studies department: research is an essential component of historical study. There are also assured exercises in other departments that require students to conduct research, and librarians support the students and their teachers during those experiences too.

Research is a process, and, sadly, students often get through high school without practicing and learning it. They frequently approach research tasks knowing what they "want to say"—and then finding resources that support their point of view. Bias confirmation. When they do this, they miss the point of research altogether, which is to:

- Explore a concept.
- Formulate a line of inquiry out of initial discoveries.

- Deepen knowledge by investigating multiple perspectives on the subject.
- Document developing learning.
- Synthesize learning into an original idea.
- Articulate and publish that idea.
- Incorporate new learning into their knowledge base for reflection and future retrieval and consultation.

This is why Sarah Maslin Nir said to hold your thesis lightly. Be open to having your ideas and presumptions challenged, and be willing to let go of them or modify them in the face of evidence. Teaching students to navigate the research process—by shifting their search strategies and resource types from reference to more granular publications such as scholarly research, statistical data, and primary sources—will help students master the critical thinking skills required to sniff out manipulative information and untruths. The research process demands inquiry, curiosity, skepticism, and some degree of ingenuity.

To this end, much time, research, critical thought, and reflection have been dedicated to creating this research model, which was adapted from Barbara Stripling's Model of Inquiry developed in 2003. The main stages of the research process we coach (Wonder, Investigate, Synthesize, Express, Review [WISER]) are paired with check points (which serve as formative assessments). For each stage, the wheel describes the relevant processes and types of resources that apply. There is also a guiding question for each stage to help students gauge their focus. This cyclical process is divided into five stages and illustrated by the WISER infographic in Figure 5.1.

Stripling's work continues, and her Information Fluency Continuum, developed in 2010 (also known as Empire State Information Fluency Continuum), blends inquiry with student aesthetic growth and social responsibility. This updated exploration of information literacy standards emphasizes how critical the endurance of inquiry skills underpinning all curricula is as our sources of information evolve and expand (New York City).

WONDER

Wonder is the initial stage of research. During this phase, student researchers define their topic and write a research question that is manageable within the parameters of their assignment. Can this question be answered in four or five pages? If not, can you narrow your focus geographically? By time period? By focusing on a certain population demographic? A student starts with a question such as, "In what ways has the evolution of media and the public's ability to gain insight into the actions of the government and president through new technology impacted the popularity of an administration at any time?" The student then hones the focus to the question: "How did the creation and widespread use of television influence the public's perspective of candidates Nixon and Kennedy, as they battled for voters in the race to be the 35th president of the United States?" A student could start with a question like this:

FIGURE 5.1   Research Continuum.

"How has public knowledge and interest in civil rights and discrimination changed from the post–Civil War era to the time of Martin Luther King Jr. to today?" And that question could be reshaped and sharpened like this: "How did public perception of African Americans' roles in society lead to the pseudo legality of the Jim Crow practice of lynching?"

Once students have defined the scope of their topic and crafted a succinct and manageable question to guide their research, they can proceed with initial source searching. If the students are engaged in authentic inquiry, they have given themselves permission to contemplate a topic about which they don't know very much but in which they are interested. Thus, this phase is characterized by the reading of reference material and then the generation of a list of keywords that can be used to dig deeper into different aspects of the topic; these keywords can be dates and proper nouns (people, places, titles of legislation, etc.).

INVESTIGATE

Students are ready to investigate once they have collected an exhaustive list of key terms. It is time to move beyond the general knowledge reference resources and begin examining books, news stories, and more in-depth and analytical texts. At this point, students are consulting a range of media. Classroom teachers sometimes direct students to include particular sources such as *New York Times* articles, TED talks, e-books, and other such media in their research. The school librarian can work with students to develop effective search strategies, including:

- Boolean operators (AND, OR, NOT).
- Truncation (edu* searches for education, educational, educate, educators).
- Wild cards (wom?n searches for women and woman).
- Database limiters like date, geography, and source type.

At this point in the process, it is important to show students how these search techniques work in Google searches, as well as other Google tips and tricks like using the delimiter "site:" to tell Chrome to search a particular website, "filetype:" to search for a particular document extensions (.pdf, for example), and Google Advanced Search, which works like a database search interface. With each project, be sure to remind students that the goal of savvy searching is not to enter terms that return 10,000 results but to refine their terms and use different search limiters to reduce those results to ten or so that pointedly address different aspects of the question they are asking. Copious search results mean there is much information related to topic; the challenge to the researcher is using appropriate tools to cull through the information and distill it to the essential, valuable elements.

When students embark on the investigate phase, they benefit from graphic organizers that help them unpack and sort the information they find. Tools such as the Research Journal Template serve many purposes for the student, the teacher, and the school librarians. At the top of each entry to the journal, students create the MLA 8 citation for the source they are unpacking so that the teacher and librarian can check their citations early in the process. Next, students put the source through the SLAP test: summarize the source, explain what you learned, and describe how you will apply it to answering your research question. You might be familiar with the CRAAP test (more on this process in the lessons portion of this book); that is the next portion of the research journal entry so that students explain the source's credibility. Finally, they enter specific notes from the source: facts, statistics, data, expert opinion, and the like. (See the Research Journal document on page 000; duplicate this page for each source consulted.)

When the student, teacher, and librarian review the entries into these journals, they are able to identify gaps in questioning, in source identification and location, and in content understanding. They are valuable formative assessments and organizational tools.

SYNTHESIZE

In this stage, students are beginning to answer their research question. They are reviewing the information they have found, examining it for gaps (and then filling them), and then drafting their thesis. The key to this stage is helping students to understand that a research paper is not a summary of readings

Research Journal

My research question:

MLA 8 Citation:

Summarize, Learn, Apply		
Summarize the source.	What did you learn?	How will you apply this?
Circle 2–3 from the list below: **C**urrency—Is it up-to-date, and does that matter? **R**elevance—How does this help me? **A**uthority—Who wrote it? **A**ccuracy—Is it verifiable? **P**urpose—Why was it written?	Which two parts of the CRAAP test does your resource best meet? Explain your choices in 2–3 sentences:	

List evidence from this source. key facts/statistics, expert opinions, or personal anecdotes
Note 1:
Note 2:
Note 3:
Note 4:
Note 5:

Answering my research questions How are the notes above helping you answer your research questions? What do you understand about your topic because of the information in this source?

Duplicate this page for each source you consult.

From *News Literacy: The Keys to Combating Fake News* by Michelle Luhtala and Jacquelyn Whiting. Santa Barbara, CA: Libraries Unlimited. Copyright © 2018

Planning My Paper

My research question (what I have been wondering):

My thesis (what I can prove):

Idea 1:	Idea 2:	Idea 3:
Topic sentence:	Topic sentence:	Topic sentence:
Evidence 1a: Source citation:	Evidence 2a: Source citation:	Evidence 3a: Source citation:
Evidence 1b: Source citation:	Evidence 2b: Source citation:	Evidence 3b: Source citation:
Evidence 1c: Source citation:	Evidence 2c: Source citation:	Evidence 3c: Source citation:

Conclusion (why what I have proved matters):

From *News Literacy: The Keys to Combating Fake News* by Michelle Luhtala and Jacquelyn Whiting. Santa Barbara, CA: Libraries Unlimited. Copyright © 2018

presented in chronological order or according to some other imposed structure. Synthesis requires students to examine their research question and their thesis in order to break down that idea into individual components that require examination, and this examination is carefully crafted to prove the thesis. Each idea is developed through a discussion of a combination of the resources the student analyzed.

The graphic organizer on page 000 (Planning My Paper) can help students visualize what synthesis is and how to organize their research writing or argument creation.

EXPRESS

Let the writing, or filming, or designing begin! At this point, as students are composing their product, provide instruction about author attribution. Instruction focuses on these questions: How do you know when you should refer to an expert when introducing a source quotation? What makes someone an expert? (See Figure 5.2.)

This is the time to teach or review protocols for formatting in-text citations (embedded references) and to give feedback on students' works cited (more on this in Chapter 7). The formative assessment for this step in the process is the

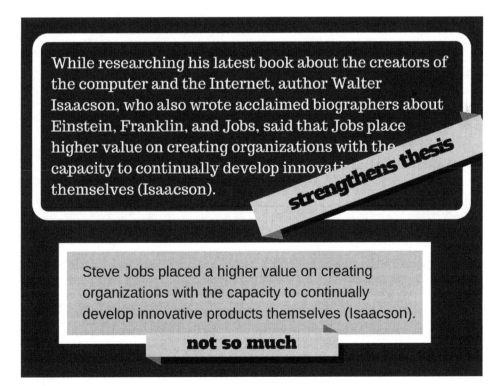

FIGURE 5.2 Expert Attribution.

outline, storyboard, plan, or preliminary draft that the student creates for review and feedback by peers, the teacher, and/or the school librarian.

REVIEW

Students' metacognitive review of their process and product is key to progress. Following are copious questions that can be used to guide students' thoughtful consideration of how they approach a task, what they are learning, where they are struggling, and what strategies they do and can employ. In Chapter 10, you can find rubrics for helping students monitor and improve their reflection.

Regarding Time Management
- How do you schedule your homework? How can you fit regular writing sessions into that plan? Would writing days in class be helpful to you, or are they not productive time?
- How can you capitalize on meeting, conferencing, and collaboration in order to get the input or inspiration that will help you?

About Reading Strategies
- How is the content reading going?
- Have you learned anything (content or process) from your secondary source reading and primary document examinations?
- When you read, *how* did you read?
- Do you print out the documents or read them online?
- What did you do to prepare to read them? How did you know what to look for or focus on?
- If you printed them out, did you have paper to make notes on while and after you read?
- If you read them online, did you copy them into a file where you could annotate them, such as Google Docs?
- If you highlight, is it just to keep your eyes focused on the page? How do you know what to highlight?
- What do you write down? What questions do you ask? What do you write about when you finish reading?
- If the document is long, do you read it in sections? What do you do at the end of each section?

Consider Your Writing Strategies
- How do you approach first drafts?
- What are you confident about? What are you concerned about? Confused about?
- How do you approach revisions? What worked? What didn't?
- In preparation for writing, how do you collect your thoughts, ideas, and questions?
- Do you free-write? How do you go about it?
- How do you choose a topic?

- How do you organize your ideas once they are collected?
- Why do you think these strategies are working?
- If they aren't working as well as you think they could, what concerns do you have? Where do you need help or suggestions?
- What are your strengths and weaknesses as a writer and thinker? Are you a strong thinker but not so good at the follow-through? Are you best at the big picture or the details? Are you a last-minute writer, or do you plan things out and stick to the plan?
- Do you start relatively early or relatively late in the time frame given for completing a task? Do you go through several early drafts, or do you simply work on your text once and then turn it in?
- How well do you understand the written and verbal comments that have been provided to you? What do these comments tell you about yourself as a writer and thinker? What do you do about comments you don't understand?
- What advice have you solicited to help you develop as a writer and thinker? What was/were the source(s) of this advice? What advice have you been given?
- What advice have you accepted? Rejected? Why?
- Describe the major changes that you made on your writing so far. Provide a rationale for why you have made these changes.
- How has the revision process allowed you to *see* content, in general, in a more sophisticated manner?
- How have the writing and thinking that you have been asked to do in the past prepared you for the kinds of writing and thinking that you have been asked to do for this class?
- What are your goals for your next piece of writing? Where do those goals come from?

Questions about Critical Thinking
- What are the major content/critical thinking/writing issues that you have been confronted with in this class?
- How well do you understand the content/substance of what you have been writing and thinking about for this class?
- What has been your plan or strategy in addressing these issues in this class? Was this plan similar to the plans you have used in the past? How and why did you know those steps would work? Is your plan working?
- What do you think your main goals should be as a thinker, given what you have experienced so far in this class? Why are these your goals?
- What are your criteria for quality work? What areas of the rubrics are still unclear to you? How are you attempting to reach clarity about these areas?
- What was the most important thing you have learned about yourself as a thinker so far?

Regarding a Particular Task Already Completed
- Did you understand what this assignment was asking you to do?
- Where did you start? How did it end?

- What obstacles did you run into?
- Did you ever move in a different direction? Did that help?
- What did you do when you did not understand?
- Was your process successful?
- Was your finished product successful?
- What would you do differently and/or keep the same?

Regarding an Imminent Task or One Underway

- What obstacles are you running into?
- How am I doing?
- Am I on the right track?
- How should I proceed?
- What information is important to remember?
- Should I move in a different direction?
- Should I adjust the pace depending on the difficulty?
- What do I need to do if I do not understand?
- Was my plan successful?
- Was my finished product successful?
- What would I do differently and/or keep the same?
- What do I know?
- What don't I know?
- What do I need to know?
- How do I find out what I know?
- How do I monitor my progress?
- What is my plan?
- How do I know if my plan is not working?
- What do I do when I get stuck?
- What would I do differently and/or keep the same?

Regarding Long-Term Projects

- Basically (give your initial response), how did the project go?
- How would you describe the process of working on a major project like this for an extended period of time?
- What were the positives?
- What were the challenges?
- How did you overcome these challenges?
- In the end, how do you feel about the project? Personally? As a learning experience?
- If it was a group project, what was your major role in completing this project?
- How did you know what this role was?
- Did this role change? Why did it change?
- Did you find your role difficult? If you had trouble, how did you reach solutions?
- Describe your work habits during this project. Did they evolve or change?
- Which worked best? Worst?
- Were the circumstances right for success?
- What factors could you control, and what was outside of your control?

- Can you change these conditions for success?
- Describe your dedication to this project.
- What was the major source of motivation?
- In comparison to other learning experiences, how does this project compare?
- What did you do well? What did your group do well?
- What could you have done better?
- What could the group have done better?
- Were you disciplined with yourself?
- Did you and your group succeed?
- Did you celebrate your success?
- How does your success on this task represent an advance from previous tasks?
- What was your most valuable experience with this task?
- For your next task, what strategies will you take with you?
- Does your grade reflect your (and your group's) achievement?
- How else do/can you measure your success on this activity?

You might be wondering what is the connection between these metacognitive habits of mind and information literacy? Students who thoughtfully and purposefully consider how and why they work as they do will also wonder about how and why others do what they do. These students will approach information or the products of other people's work with healthy skepticism, naturally asking, "What is this? Why was it created? Who participated? What compromises were made? What shortcuts might have been taken? What did someone stand to gain by creating the text this way? Did someone else stand to lose something?"—and other questions key to understanding the news they consume.

REFERENCE

New York City School Library System. "Empire State Information Fluency Continuum." New York City Department of Education. Accessed May 18, 2017. schools.nyc.gov/NR/rdonlyres/1A931D4E-1620-4672-ABEF-460A273D 0D5F/0/EmpireStateIFC.pdf.

6

Lessons for Developing Information Literacy

DEVELOPING RESEARCH QUESTIONS

Research is the backbone of inquiry-based learning, and the research question is the backbone of research. Students define their topic, the scope of their research, and the basis of their thesis with their research question. Learning to ask an insightful, unique question that is focused enough to match the parameters of their task is an essential research skill. As pedagogy shifts to become increasingly student centered, more and more high-quality resources are becoming available. One of these is the approach developed and described by the Right Question Institute in their publication, *Make Just One Change* (Rothstein and Santana). If you are not familiar with the Question Formulation Technique (QFT) that they developed, it is worth reading! You can also find, on social media, many educators discussing how they implemented QFT class exercises for numerous aspects of inquiry. It can be particularly helpful with students who are developing research questions (more on this in Lesson 2).

Lesson 1: Question Stems

When working with students on research exercises, begin with lessons designed to help them with the development of their research questions. The scope of their research and the means by which they explore what they learn are products of a well crafted research question. Students have a tendency to ask very narrow questions that begin with "what" and very broad questions that begin with "why." Without prompting and practice, they get stuck here: too narrow or too broad. To help them expand their inquiry strategies, provide these question stems to push their thinking:

Which? This stem helps you to collect information to make an informed choice.

For example: Which 20th-century president did the most to promote civil rights? Which Civil War general was the best military strategist? Which of the characters in *Henry IV, Part 1* has the most relevance for today's politicians?

How? When you seek to understand problems and perspectives, weigh options, and propose solutions, try starting your question with this stem.

For example: How should we solve the problem of water pollution in Long Island Sound? How did King Cotton affect the Confederacy's waging of war? In *Henry IV, Part 1*, how does Hal's ascension to the throne affect perceptions of his father's coup? How can child soldiers be rehabilitated?

What if? Your question can change history! Use the knowledge you have to pose a hypothesis and consider options.

For example: What if the Apollo 13 Astronauts had not survived? What if General Lee had better intelligence at Gettysburg? What if Brutus had made the final funeral oration in *Julius Caesar*?

Should? A question can invite self- or community examination. Using this stem, you can make a moral or practical decision based on evidence.

For example: Should we clone humans? Should Confederate symbols be used in official state flags and logos today? Should Hamlet have minded his own business?

Why? Understand and explain relationships to get to the essence of a complicated issue.

For example: Why do people engage in human trafficking? Why did Great Britain favor the South during the Civil War? Why does Shakespeare use so many references to the natural and unnatural in Macbeth?

These stems are valuable because students can decide on the purpose of their inquiry and use the stem best suited to that end. They also are versatile and can be used in any discipline. Notice that the sample questions cover history, current events, and literature; they can easily be cultural or scientific in focus as well. What is really key is that they push students away from bias confirmation, away from the tendency to ask questions to which they believe they already know the right answer. By using these stems and asking many questions about the same topic, they are pushed to think critically about the subject of their research and remain open to a range of evidence and perspectives before developing their thesis. Provide an organizer like this to help the students expand their thinking about their topic:

My topic:	Question 1	Question 2
Which one? Collect information to make an informed choice.		
How? Understand problems and perspectives, weigh options, and propose solutions.		
What if? Use the knowledge you have to pose a hypothesis and consider options.		
Should? Make a moral or practical decision based on evidence.		
Why? Understand and explain relationships to get to the essence of a complicated issue.		

From *News Literacy: The Keys to Combating Fake News* by Michelle Luhtala and Jacquelyn Whiting. Santa Barbara, CA: Libraries Unlimited. Copyright © 2018

These stems can help students focus their research topics under the umbrella of a unit essential question. For example, suppose the unit essential question is, "What should America's response be to the current refugee crisis?" Imagine the research possibilities with each of the following stems: "Which country has a fair, enforceable policy in the current refugee crisis?" "How does the U.S. response to Syrian refugees compare with the U.S. response to Holocaust/Bosnian/Vietnamese refugees?" "What if the United States reinstated quotas like those of the 1920s?" "Should the UN establish and monitor camps for the refugees?" "Why did the French respond to the Calais Jungle as they did?" Using these question stems, the students can focus their research on the aspect of this issue that is most interesting to them, and the teacher can engage with the students about content that the student has chosen so that the curricular experience is personalized. Ultimately, in this exercise, students can write op-ed pieces based on what they learned, and the range of issues and perspectives they consider can lead to rich classroom discussion. And, the classroom teacher has the added benefit of not having to read 25 identical papers!

If resources permit, an extension of this exercise is the creation of a website to which the students can post their op-ed essays. In so doing, they create their own newspaper editorial section, which can be public to the school, the district, or the world and can invite comments so that the students are engaged in a community dialogue beyond their teacher and the classroom.

Lesson 2: The QFT

This lesson was adapted from the protocols developed by the Right Question Institute and described in their publication, *Make Just One Change* (Rothstein and Santana). Working with students preparing to write their first major research paper in high school—and a high-stakes paper because successful completion of the paper is a graduation requirement—is an intensive process that affords extended coteaching time in many classes. Prior to beginning this process, students had read *The Great Gatsby* and examined that text under the unit essential question, "How does socioeconomic status impact opportunity in the United States?" Rather than have the entire class work from one so-called Q-focus (the artifact that will inspire their question brainstorming), we provided multiple artifacts and allowed the students to choose the one with which they wanted to work. Their options were:

- An expired U.S. green card.
- Excerpts regarding free and reduced lunch, testing, discipline, and other data from a strategic school profile for a nearby high school.
- A graph showing educational disparities between husbands and wives broken down by race.
- A bilingual Mexican-issued birth certificate for a person born in Mexico to a U.S. national.
- A photo of the St. Louis Rams football team walking to the field with their hands raised (the pose of the hands-up-don't-shoot protests).
- A chart comparing household income and race.
- A graph comparing health care access and income.

We outlined the QFT process on Google Slides so that students could crowd source questions for each prompt before sorting them into groups of closed and open questions. Using this basic tech tool facilitated collaboration and allowed for reflection on and subsequent revision of the questions to suit the needs of individual students. According to the QFT protocol, they rewrote closed questions to be open (see Figure 6.1) and open questions to be closed (see Figure 6.2).

Students posted all of this thinking on Google Slides. Sharing their thinking on Google Slides made it easy for us to collaborate with the classroom teachers when reviewing the students' ideas, as well as allowing the students to see how they were each approaching the task and the subject matter. Ultimately, each group chose their three best questions to post to a final slide. The criterion for being one of the best questions was "questions that your group thinks best expose an important element of a potential research topic." The librarians collaborated with the classroom teachers to review the questions, provide feedback, and help students adopt and revise a question to suit their interests.

REFERENCE

Rothstein, Dan, and Luz Santana. *Make Just One Change*. Cambridge, MA: Harvard Education Press, 2011.

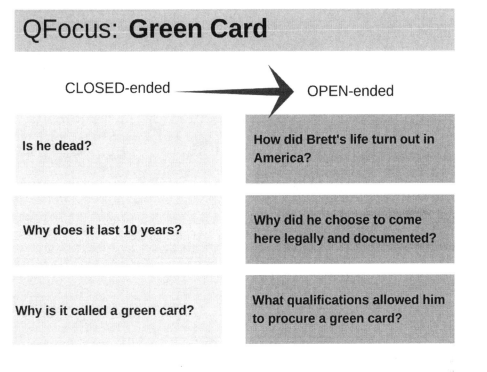

FIGURE 6.1 Green Card.

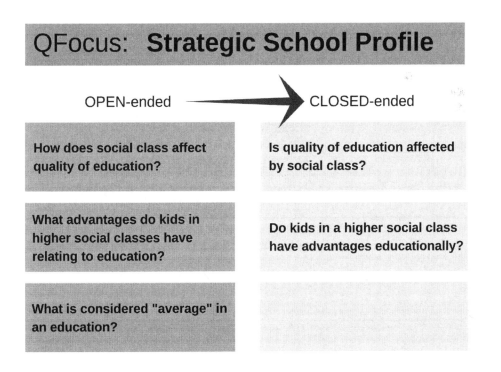

FIGURE 6.2 Strategic School Profile.

RECOGNIZING AND ACCOUNTING FOR BIAS

Students frequently ask, "Can you help me find a source that's not biased?" Asking that question indicates that the students need to learn that (1) there are degrees of bias and (2) everyone has bias, so (3) there is no such thing as an unbiased source. Instead, content teachers and school librarians need to teach students to recognize what a text creator's bias is and how or whether that bias negates the usefulness of that source for the student's purpose. In essence, students must learn to engage with varying bias and points of view, not avoid them.

Lesson 3: What Is My Bias?

Teaching students to recognize their own biases is an essential step in the process of guiding them toward becoming savvy consumers of information. When students ask for help finding a source that is "unbiased," they signal that they don't understand what bias is. They must learn to wrestle with and account for bias in their own research and writing. This means recognizing their own outlooks first so that they can read and view critically, with an open mind to new intellectual possibilities.

In some schools, students (particularly high school students) are assigned research papers that are benchmark assessments. Frequently, successful completion of these assessments is a graduation requirement. Purposefully providing these students mentor texts connected to the content they are studying and practicing the unpacking of these texts pay dividends when the students begin to work independently on their research. This sample exercise is based on the conducting of research during a unit on the relationship between socioeconomic status and educational experience, so this topic informs the mentor text being used. To facilitate the students' resource selection and understanding of the impact of bias on source credibility, they can start unpacking an editorial from the "Room for Debate" section of the *New York Times* in response to the question: "Is School Reform Hopeless?" (Carter) This exercise can easily be modified and adapted to any other content focus by selecting an alternative model essay.

This exercise is scaffolded to help students begin to understand their own biases on a topic and how those biases will influence how they understand what they read and how they convey what they ultimately write. In fact, they must learn to recognize how their bias informs their word choices when developing keyword lists for researching. In other words, how does their bias impact the information they consume and the knowledge they create? From the selected editorial, for the first portion of the lesson, students will consider just the conclusion. Words have been selectively removed from the paragraph so that students can replace the blanks with whatever word they think best conveys the meaning of the paragraph. Ask them to complete this exercise individually and then partner with two or three other students in the class to compile their words on one document and to compare how they each completed the paragraph and how their choice of words changed the meaning of the paragraph. By enlarging the paragraph to a poster size, students can write their words on Post-it® notes and hang their paragraph on the classroom wall so that each group can circulate and review how their classmates completed the exercise.

Here is an example of a phrase with blanks to be filled:

[T]oo many are climbing stairwells with broken handrails and missing steps, tripping and falling as they _____ to keep up, while others are _____ up on elevators.

Consider these possible ways to complete the sentence:

- **struggling** to keep up, while others are **racing** up
- **trying** to keep up, while others are **rising** up
- **attempting** to keep up, while others are **moving** up

In a class discussion, students might observe that "racing" implies competition, "rising" implies progress and maybe increase in status, while "moving" is more passive. They might be surprised that none of those are the words that the author used!

The actual sentence is, "[T]oo many are climbing stairwells with broken handrails and missing steps, tripping and falling as they **work** to keep up, while others are **zooming** up on elevators."

Certainly "working" implies a conscious sense of purpose and purposefulness to the effort that is not reflected in "struggle," "try," or "attempt." "Work" may also imply a degree of success and ability absent in those other terms. "Zooming" also has a very different connotation than the words the students chose, particularly in contrast to "working." Ask students to compare their bias with that of the author and consider how differing opinions might influence their assessment of the source's credibility.

For the next phase of this exercise, provide the students with the rest of the editorial with highlighted words or phrases and added questions in order to invite students to discuss the writer's choice of words and how those words affected the meaning of her editorial.

Here is an example paragraph:

> In addition to attending to these **basic survival needs**, schools have to attract experienced teachers and leaders with the **right sensibilities** and training to educate youth from diverse social and cultural backgrounds. Successful school districts also enhance **youth development** through extracurricular activities and additional enrichment. When families cannot afford costly after-school programs, personal tutors and experiential summer vacations, effective school-communities invest in programs to offset these **opportunity gaps**.

Here are the questions that could be posed corresponding to each of the highlighted phrases:

1. What does the phrase "basic survival needs" imply?
2. What do you think "right sensibilities" are?
3. How is "youth development" different from education?
4. What other "opportunity gaps" have you heard of?

As students share their conclusions and questions, they may raise further word choice questions like: "What does equity mean?" This is a great opportunity to direct students to the Allsides Dictionary. Here is how Allsides describes their dictionary:

> A human look at hot-button terms from every perspective: Controversial terms, from "abortion" to "Zionism", tend to shut down dialog because they mean different things to different people. Until we fully understand what a term means to someone else, we don't know the issue and can't effectively communicate.

Visit their site (Allsides.com/dictionary/equity) to see how Allsides defines "equity" and the cartoon they use to distinguish "equity" from "equality." The resources provided by Allsides are incredibly valuable to students as they learn to navigate the information they encounter and develop information literacy—particularly in the face of fake news!

REFERENCES

"AllSides Dictionary." *AllSides*. Accessed May 18, 2017. http://allsides.com/dictionary.

Carter, Prudence L. "Poor Schools Need to Encompass More Than Instruction to Succeed." *New York Times*, September 14, 2016. http://nytimes.com/roomfor debate/2016/09/14/is-school-reform-hopeless/poor-schools-need-to-encom pass-more-than-instruction-to-succeed.

CONSIDERING PRIMARY SOURCES

As students progress through the research process, their source focus becomes increasingly granular. They leave behind the reference sources with which they began the process and apply what they learned from those sources to more scholarly and primary texts.

Lesson 4: Primary Source Close Reading

The same pedagogy that informs the lesson on detecting one's own bias can be applied to primary sources as well: provide students with the primary source with identifying words removed and ask them to work individually to complete the document in a certain context and then compare the results with one another and the original. Doing this to introduce a unit is a valuable way to have students recognize their assumptions so that they can confront how those assumptions might interfere with their understanding of a person, place, or time different from their own. Or, after engaging in part of the unit study, ask students to fill in the blanks to try to determine the context and author. Yet another approach is to turn the document into a Madlibs-style exercise by indicating the part of the speech of each of the missing words.

Possible Documents
- "Ain't I A Woman?" by Sojourner Truth (modeled on page 000):
- "The Meaning of the 4th of July to the Negro" by Frederick Douglass (excerpted):
  http://jackiewhiting.net/AmStudies/Units1314/Liberty/Douglass
      .html
- Lincoln's 2nd Inaugural Address:
  https://www.ourdocuments.gov/doc.php?flash=true&doc=38
- The Truman Doctrine:
  https://www.ourdocuments.gov/doc.php?flash=true&doc=81
- "Remember the Ladies" by Abigail Adams:
  https://founders.archives.gov/documents/Adams/04-01-02-0241

Also consider songs or less well-known documents like personal letters.

Model Document (full text below)

Delivered in _____ (date)

_____ Convention, _____ (location)

Well, _____, where there is so much racket there must be something out of kilter. I think that _____ the _____ of the _____ and the women at the _____, all talking about rights, the _____ will be in a fix pretty soon. But what's all this here _____ about?

That man over there says that _____ need to be _____ into _____, and lifted over _____, and to have the best place everywhere. Nobody ever helps me into _____, or over _____, or gives me any best place! And _____ I a _____? Look at me! Look at my arm! I have ploughed and planted, and gathered into barns, and no m_____an could _____ me! And _____ I a _____? I could work as much and eat as much as a _____—when I could get it—and bear the _____ as well! And _____ I a _____? I have borne _____ _____, and seen most all _____ off to _____, and when I cried out with my mother's grief, none but _____ heard me! And _____ I a _____?

Then they talk about this thing in the head; what's this they call it? [member of audience whispers, "_____"] That's it, honey. What's that got to do with _____ _____ or _____ rights? If my cup won't hold but a pint, and yours holds a quart, wouldn't you be mean not to let me have my little half measure full?

Then that little man in black there, he says _____ can't have as much rights as _____, 'cause _____ wasn't a _____! Where did your Christ come from? Where did your Christ come from? From God and a woman! _____ had nothing to do with Him.

If the first woman God ever made was strong enough to turn the world upside down all alone, these women together ought to be able to turn it back, and get it right side up again! And now they is asking to do it, the _____ better let them.

Obliged to you for hearing me, and now old Sojourner ain't got nothing more to say.

From *News Literacy: The Keys to Combating Fake News* by Michelle Luhtala and Jacquelyn Whiting. Santa Barbara, CA: Libraries Unlimited. Copyright © 2018

Full Text

Sojourner Truth (1797–1883): Ain't I A Woman?
Delivered 1851

Women's Convention, Akron, Ohio

Well, children, where there is so much racket there must be something out of kilter. I think that 'twixt the negroes of the South and the women at the North, all talking about rights, the white men will be in a fix pretty soon. But what's all this here talking about?

That man over there says that women need to be helped into carriages, and lifted over ditches, and to have the best place everywhere. Nobody ever helps me into carriages, or over mud-puddles, or gives me any best place! And ain't I a woman? Look at me! Look at my arm! I have ploughed and planted, and gathered into barns, and no man could head me! And ain't I a woman? I could work as much and eat as much as a man—when I could get it—and bear the lash as well! And ain't I a woman? I have borne thirteen children, and seen most all sold off to slavery, and when I cried out with my mother's grief, none but Jesus heard me! And ain't I a woman?

Then they talk about this thing in the head; what's this they call it? [member of audience whispers, "intellect"] That's it, honey. What's that got to do with women's rights or negroes' rights? If my cup won't hold but a pint, and yours holds a quart, wouldn't you be mean not to let me have my little half measure full?

Then that little man in black there, he says women can't have as much rights as men, 'cause Christ wasn't a woman! Where did your Christ come from? Where did your Christ come from? From God and a woman! Man had nothing to do with Him.

If the first woman God ever made was strong enough to turn the world upside down all alone, these women together ought to be able to turn it back, and get it right side up again! And now they is asking to do it, the men better let them.

Obliged to you for hearing me, and now old Sojourner ain't got nothing more to say.

Lesson 5: Text, Context, and Subtext in Primary Sources

Graphic organizers are excellent tools for guiding student inquiry, creating formative assessment checkpoints, and pacing student work so that they are thoughtful and thorough in their source examination. Here are some examples of graphic organizers that support students' analysis of various types of sources. Notice that a common component, regardless of the type of source being examined, is that first students make observations, then they pose questions, and finally respond to open-ended questions.

Declaration of Independence

TEXT: *What is this document?*	
July 4, 1776	**CONTEXT**: When and why was it written? By whom? For whom? And, about whom?
When in the course of human events, it becomes necessary for **one people** to dissolve the political bands which have connected them with **another**, and to assume among the powers of the earth, the separate and equal station to which the **laws of nature** and of **nature's God** entitle them, a decent respect to the opinions of *mankind* requires that they should declare the causes which impel them to the separation. **We** hold these *truths* to be self-evident:	**SUBTEXT:** What is being said without overtly saying it? What do the words in bold tell you about the authors' intentions? What do you wonder about the author and the audience?
That all *men* are *created* equal; that they are endowed by their Creator with certain unalienable rights; that among these are life, liberty, and the pursuit of happiness; that, to secure these rights, governments are instituted among men, deriving their *just* powers from the consent of the governed; that whenever any form of government becomes destructive of these ends, it is the right of the people to alter or to abolish it, and to institute new government, laying its foundation on such principles, and organizing its powers in such form, as to them shall seem most likely to affect their *safety* and *happiness*. Prudence, indeed, will dictate that governments long established should not be changed for light and transient causes; and accordingly all experience hath shown that mankind are more disposed to suffer, while evils are sufferable than to right themselves by abolishing the forms to which they are accustomed. But when a long train of abuses and usurpations, pursuing invariably the same object, evinces a design to reduce them under absolute despotism, it is their right, it is their *duty*, to throw off such government, and to provide new guards for their future security. Such has been the patient sufferance of these colonies; and such is now the necessity which constrains them to alter their former systems of government. The history of the present King of Great Britain is a history of repeated injuries and usurpations, all having in direct object the establishment of an absolute *tyranny* over these states. To prove this, let facts be submitted to a candid world. . . .	**SUBTEXT:** What is being said without overtly saying it? What is the PURPOSE of GOVERNMENT? What are the RIGHTS and RESPONSIBILITIES of the RULERS and the RULED?

From *News Literacy: The Keys to Combating Fake News* by Michelle Luhtala and Jacquelyn Whiting. Santa Barbara, CA: Libraries Unlimited. Copyright © 2018

In this next exercise, students are asked to compare the context in which a document was created with today's context. Doing so helps students understand how point of view can vary from person to person and from time to time, which means that even when one person uses the same vocabulary as another person, those people don't always mean the same thing. Following the document organizer are reflection and discussion questions that invite students to embrace the changing meaning of different concepts.

The Preamble to the U.S. Constitution

We the people of the United States,

in order to form a more perfect union,	
1789	Today

establish justice,	
1789	Today

insure domestic tranquility,	
1789	Today

provide for the common defense,	
1789	Today

promote the general welfare,	
1789	Today

and secure the blessings of liberty to ourselves and our posterity,	
1789	Today

do ordain and establish this Constitution for the United States of America

- Has the purpose of the national government changed in this new constitution?
- What is it now? How do you know?
- How do you think the weaknesses of the Articles will be addressed in the Constitution?
- Which of the values expressed in the Preamble is most important to you? Why?

From *News Literacy: The Keys to Combating Fake News* by Michelle Luhtala and Jacquelyn Whiting. Santa Barbara, CA: Libraries Unlimited. Copyright © 2018

Understanding Constitutional Amendments and the Court (More Primary Sources)

This exercise asks students to practice strategies for close reading of a text in which the content, vocabulary, or sentence structure will be unfamiliar and a possible impediment to the students' understanding of the meaning of the document. It could easily be adapted to a variety of texts. After completing each step in the following outline, students should share their work with the classroom teacher and library media specialist for feedback before proceeding to the next step. Notice that this process uses a flipped classroom model in that students are provided video resources to help them with the content and requires students to collaborate and compare their insights. Rubrics for each of the assessment ideas are available in Chapter 10.

Step I: Unpacking the Text

1. Silently read the amendment you are examining and highlight words you don't know. Define those words in the following space.

2. Read the Amendment out loud. Review the words you didn't know the first time. Read it a third time and highlight the key parts.

3. Watch the video (the Hip Hughes YouTube channel has short videos on each amendment) and take notes in this space.

4. Write a summary of the amendment in your own words.

Share with teacher and library media specialist!

Step II: Extending the Text

1. Brainstorm questions that this text raises for you. Write them here:

2. Share your list with at least one other person who is examining the same amendment.

3. Capture any new ideas and questions that emerge from this conversation.

4. Sort and organize your questions:

Broad, inferencing questions:	Fact-based questions:
Pair the fact questions with the inferencing questions they help to answer.	

5. Choose one of your inferencing questions to guide your analysis of the amendment.

Share with teacher and library media specialist again!

Step III: Source Location

1. Search Facts on File* (LMC Database) in the Issues and Controversies section for a secondary source about the subject of your question. References books are collected in the LMC that you also may use to locate this source.

MLA 8 Citation:

2. Find two editorials about your amendment question: one should be a political cartoon, the other a written commentary. *(Lessons 11–13 focus on different forms of editorials.)*

MLA 8 Citation:

3. Find another primary source about your amendment question. You can use a database or a purposeful Google search to find this source.

MLA 8 Citation:

4. Find one Supreme Court case that addresses your amendment (Oyez.org).

MLA 8 Citation:

Share a third time!

Step IV: Answering Your Question

- Read the sources you collected and take notes on all information and ideas that address your question. For this step, you may start a new Google doc onto which you copy your questions.
- Determine the best medium or format for presenting your answer to your question:
  - Create an infographic that explores the nuances of your question and research (try Canva, Google Slides or Draw, Piktochart, Visually or Infogram).
  - Record a podcast of a debate about or discussion of your question.
  - Curate a documentary video that explores your question and answer (try WeVideo, Spark, or Moovly).
  - Write an analytical essay in response to your question.
  - Write a letter to the editor or blog post about your question and answer.

From *News Literacy: The Keys to Combating Fake News* by Michelle Luhtala and Jacquelyn Whiting. Santa Barbara, CA: Libraries Unlimited. Copyright © 2018

Lesson 6: Agree and Disagree with Primary Source Authors

Another way to help students understand how their biases or information filters impact their understanding of a text or resource is to find, explore, and explain points of agreement or disagreement they have with the author. Here is that concept applied to Abigail Adams's letter to John, "Remember the Ladies," and his response; it is derived from *They Say/I Say* by Gerald Graff and Cathy Birkenstein about strategies for teaching academic writing.

The Correspondence of Abigail and John Adams on Power

Abigail Adams to John Adams, March 31, 1776

I have sometimes been ready to think that the passion for Liberty cannot be Equally Strong in the Breasts of those who have been accustomed to deprive their fellow Creatures of theirs. Of this I am certain: that it is not founded upon the generous and Christian principal of doing to others as we would that others should do unto us.

. . . I long to hear that you have declared an independency. . . . In the new Code of Laws which I suppose it will be necessary for you to make I desire you would Remember the Ladies, and be more generous and favourable to them than your ancestors. Do not put such unlimited power into the hands of the Husbands. Remember all Men would be tyrants if they could. If particular care and attention is not paid to the Ladies we are determined to foment a Rebellion, and will not hold ourselves bounds by any Laws in which we have no voice, or Representation.

That your Sex are Naturally Tyrannical is a Truth so thoroughly established as to admit of no dispute. . . . Why then, not put it out of the power of the vicious and the Lawless to use us with cruelty and indignity with impunity . . . ? Men of sense in all ages abhor those customs which treat us only as the vassals of your sex. Regard us then as beings, placed by providence under your protection, and in imitation of the Supreme Being make use of that power for our happiness.

John Adams to Abigail Adams, April 14, 1776

As to your extraordinary Code of Laws, I cannot but laugh. We have been told that our Struggle has loosened the bands of Government everywhere. That children and Apprentices were disobedient—that schools and Colleges were grown turbulent—that Indians slighted their Guardians and Negroes grew insolent to their Masters. But your Letter was the first Intimation that another Tribe more numerous and powerful than all the rest were grown discontented. . . . Depend upon, it, We know better than to repeal our Masculine systems. . . . We have only the Name of Masters, and rather than give up this, which would completely subject Us to the Despotism of the Petticoat, I hope General Washington, and all our brave Heroes would fight.

Abigail Adams to John Adams, May 7, 1776

Arbitrary power is like most other things which are very hard, very liable to be broken.

Disagreeing Templates

Assert an alternative point of view by offering persuasive reasons why you disagree: show factors not taken into account by the original argument, highlight faulty or incomplete evidence, question the assumptions or flawed logic of another point of view.

1. John/Abigail is mistaken because he/she overlooks _____.
2. John/Abigail's claim that _____ rests upon the questionable assumption that _____.
3. I disagree with John/Abigail's view that _____ because, as recent events have shown, _____.
4. John/Abigail contradicts him-/herself. On the one hand, he/she argues _____; on the other hand, he/she also says _____.

Agreeing Templates

Support a view taken by someone else by bringing a fresh idea to the discussion: highlight new evidence, synthesize with your corroborating experience, or provide an accessible translation of an esoteric point.

1. I agree John/Abigail that power _____ because my experience with _____ confirms it.
2. John/Abigail is surely right about power because he/she may not have been aware _____.
3. John/Abigail's notion of power is extremely useful because it sheds light on the difficult problem of _____.
4. Those unfamiliar with the correspondence between John and Abigail Adams and their relationships with power may be interested to know that it basically boils down to _____.

Agree and Disagree

Show the merits and limitations of different aspects of the original argument, even stress one end of the spectrum over the other.

1. Though I concede that John/Abigail believes _____, I still insist that _____.
2. John/Abigail is right that _____, but he/she seems on more dubious ground when he/she claims that _____.
3. While John/Abigail is probably wrong when he/she claims that _____, he/she is right that _____.
4. Whereas John/Abigail provides ample evidence that _____, Abigail's/John's point on _____ convinces me that _____ instead.

5. I am of two minds about John's/Abigail's claim that _____. On the one hand, I agree that _____. On the other hand, I'm not sure if _____.

6. My feelings on the nature of power are mixed. I do support John's/Abigail's position on power that _____, but I find Abigail's/John's argument that _____ to be equally persuasive.

REFERENCE

Graff, Gerald and Cathy Birkenstein. *"They Say/I Say": The Moves That Matter in Academic Writing*. 3rd ed. New York: W. W. Norton, 2014.

Lesson 7: What *Is* This Source?

The vocabulary educators use when discussing media with students can have a subtle impact on how those students understand resources. Consider the use of the term "article" to refer to anything that appears in a newspaper or other news publication (print or digital). Perhaps this view is old school, but an article, by definition, is a straight news story. Of course, straight news is not free of bias, but the intention behind its authoring and publication is to inform—not persuade. And the advent of the digital media has expanded the types of writing that news outlets publish and what they are willing to give away for free as opposed to protect behind a paid subscription service. Straight-up news reporting by journalists is becoming increasingly proprietary—subscription based. *The Wall Street Journal* keeps almost all of its journalistic content restricted. Only blogs, columns, and opinions are accessible to the public. The *New York Times* allows nonsubscribers to access up to ten news articles per month for free. After that, a reader needs either a subscription to access more content or to wait it out until the clock resets on accessing material for free. Consequently, students, when searching for news sources online, are using opinion pieces, blogs, and columns as objective articles without realizing that they are subjective sources conveying point of view, bias, and slant. Teaching students to correctly identify the type of writing they are reading and why the publication finds value in each piece is a critical first step to students' development of information literacy.

This exercise can be successful and useful as a pen-and-paper task and is also easily convertible to a digital exercise with Google Forms and QR codes for a one-on-one environment.

All the News That's Fit to Print, and Just the Facts, Ma'am . . .

What is "straight news"? (Define it.)	In this space, insert a screen shot of a newspaper front page. Depending on your purposes, you might provide a print copy of the paper that students can hold.
When reading straight news, what do you expect to find? What are common elements of straight news stories? When you are reading something in a news source, how do you know it is straight news?	If you choose to use a digital snapshot, consider omitting the publication title and ask students to predict from which source you obtained the page.
Why do online articles have both time and date stamps?	
How is reading straight news in print different from reading it online?	

We May Not See Eye to Eye

What are the differences between editorials and op-eds?	In this space provide students with a screenshot of the opinion page from a nationally recognized publication. Be sure that your excerpt allows them to see how a publication distinguishes among columnist, editorial, contributor, and op-ed (among other possible designations). The *New York Times* is a good model for this layout.
What do these types of writing have in common?	
Where in a newspaper can you find them? Why is it not accurate to call them articles?	
Explain whether and how these essays can be used in research.	

An Article by Any Other Name Must Be a Blog

The evolution of the blog has been discussed earlier. In this space, provide students with a screenshot of a blog from a nationally recognized publication. *The Washington Post* has one that they call PostEverything. This exercise guides students to consider why a news publication would adopt this segment and what functionality it provides when reporting and commenting on the news.

What is a blog? Who can author one?	What do blogs have in common with opinion writing? How are they different?	Why do news sources dedicate a special section on their websites to blogs? Why are the writing pieces in blogs not part of the print publication?	Explain whether and how these essays can be used in research.

Now that students know *what* it is, how do they know if it is any good? On to Lesson 8!

Lesson 8: Source Evaluation

President Ronald Reagan once invoked a Russian proverb when speaking with Soviet Premier Mikhail Gorbachev. Regarding the warming relations between the two former enemy nations, Reagan famously said: *"Doveryai, no proveryai"*: "Trust, but verify." We are hoping a new library-based proverb will gain traction: Verify before Trusting. Not as sexy a saying but as important a sentiment!

That it is important to evaluate resources is a given; it is the crux of this book's purpose! But if source evaluation was easy, this book wouldn't be necessary, and people of all ages would not be duped by fake news. The CRAAP Test is a popular source evaluation tool with an easy to remember acronym for a title. As you have seen in our research journal, our students are familiar with and use the CRAAP Test. Direct students to think through the subtleties of what that tool is helping them evaluate. When evaluating sources, be sure to ask students to consider:

- **Authority:** What experience or qualifications does the author bring to this subject?
- **Purpose:** Why did the author write this?
- **Scope:** Is this work very in-depth? Does it cover a wide range of topics? How does that affect the source?
- **Audience:** For whom was it written (general public, subject specialists, students, etc.), and why does this matter?
- **Viewpoint:** What is the author's perspective or approach (school of thought, etc.)? Do you detect an unacknowledged bias or find any undefended assumptions? Is there an acknowledged bias?
- **Sources:** Does the author cite other sources? Is it based on the author's own research? Is it personal opinion? Is it substantiated? Is it convincing?
- **Conclusion:** What does the author conclude? Is the conclusion justified by the work? Are you skeptical about any parts of the work? Why?
- **Features:** Any significant extras, e.g. visual aids (charts, maps, etc.), reprints of source documents, an annotated bibliography? How do they contribute to the work?
- **Comparison:** How does it relate to other works on the topic? Does it agree or disagree with another author or a particular school of thought? Are there other works that would support or dispute it?
- **Reliability:** How do you know it is reliable source? Is it straight-up news reporting, or is it an opinion piece (blog, column, op-ed)?
- **Currency:** How up-to-date is the resource?
- **Relevance:** To what extent does the resource meet your research needs?

The CRAAP Test

Currency: *The timeliness of the information.*

- When was the information published or posted?
- Has the information been revised or updated? How can you tell?
- Does your topic require current information, or will older sources work as well?
- Are the links functional?

Relevance: *The importance of the information for your needs.*

- Does the information relate to your topic or answer your question?
- Who is the intended audience?
- Is the information at an appropriate level (i.e., not too elementary or advanced for your needs)?
- Have you looked at a variety of sources before determining this is one you will use?
- Would you be comfortable citing this source in your research paper?

Authority: *The source of the information.*

- Who is the author/publisher/source/sponsor?
- What are the author's credentials or organizational affiliations?
- Is the author qualified to write on the topic?
- Is there contact information, such as a publisher or e-mail address?
- Does the URL reveal anything about the author or source?

Accuracy: *The reliability, truthfulness, and correctness of the content.*

- Where does the information come from?
- Is the information supported by evidence?
- Has the information been reviewed or refereed?
- Can you verify any of the information in another source or from personal knowledge?
- Does the language or tone seem unbiased and free of emotion?
- Are there spelling, grammatical, or typographic errors?

Purpose: *The reason the information exists.*

- What is the purpose of the information? Is it to inform, teach, sell, entertain, or persuade?
- Do the authors/sponsors make their intentions or purpose clear?
- Is the information fact, opinion, or propaganda?
- Does the point of view appear objective and impartial?
- Are there political, ideological, cultural, religious, institutional, or personal biases?

From *News Literacy: The Keys to Combating Fake News* by Michelle Luhtala and Jacquelyn Whiting. Santa Barbara, CA: Libraries Unlimited. Copyright © 2018

Consider including a quick vocab quiz as a part of this lesson by asking students to match the keywords with their definitions. If you deliver the instruction digitally, this quiz could be part of a Nearpod lesson or a Google Form.

Match the term in the left-hand column with its appropriate definition in the right-hand column.

Relevance	An agent who contributes objective reports to a periodical publication
Currency	How a source's point of view affects the way that information is presented (Sources aren't always conscious of it.)
Reliability	A Web log on which content is published on a particular topic
Comparison	A person's perspective—how people's interests and experience shape the way they see things
Features	An agent who contributes reports to a periodical publication with expertise in a specific area and who can, when appropriate, include his/her own perspective
Conclusion	A line in a newspaper naming the writer of an article
Sources	An unsigned newspaper article written by the publication's editorial board members
	One in a regular series of newspaper or magazine articles
Viewpoint	Any significant extras, such as visual aids (charts, maps, etc.), reprints of source documents, an annotated bibliography
Audience	Breadth or depth of coverage (Is this work very in-depth? Does it cover a wide range of topics? Topics included? And so on.)
Scope	Experience or qualifications of the author
Purpose	How do you know it is trustworthy source? Is it straight-up news reporting, or is it an opinion piece (blog, column, op-ed)?
Authority	How does it relate to other works on the topic? Does it agree or disagree with another author or a particular school of thought? Are there other works that would support or dispute it?
Blog post	Any significant extras, such as visual aids (charts, maps, etc.), reprints of source documents, an annotated bibliography
Reporter	What does the author determine? Is his/her final assertion justified by the work?
Byline	Does the author cite other sources? Is it based on the author's own research? Is it personal opinion?
Column	What is the author's perspective or approach (school of thought, etc.)? Do you detect an unacknowledged bias or find any unsupported assumptions?
Correspondent	For whom was it written (general public, subject specialists, students, etc.)?
Editorial	To what extent does the resource meet your research needs?
Point of view	Why did the author write this?
Bias	A signed newspaper article that expresses the opinions of a named writer who is usually unaffiliated with the newspaper's editorial board
Op-ed	Keyword used to describe an online posting that helps users locate relevant content when searching online
Tag	How up-to-date is the resource?

From *News Literacy: The Keys to Combating Fake News* by Michelle Luhtala and Jacquelyn Whiting. Santa Barbara, CA: Libraries Unlimited. Copyright © 2018

Analyzing News Stories

Begin by selecting two stories about your assigned topic. Allsides (http://www.allsides.com) is a news aggregator that is particularly useful for this type of comparison because it offers stories from across the political spectrum that are vetted and categorized by their editorial team. The instrument they use and their backgrounds are clearly explained in their "About" section. Be sure to choose stories that will offer contrasting views.

Begin by selecting two stories about your assigned topic. Allsides is a good aggregator that offers stories from across the political spectrum. Be sure to choose stories that will offer contrasting views.

Story 1 Headline:	Story 2 Headline:
Citation:	Citation:
How effectively does the headline: 1. Summarize the story? 2. Get the reader's attention? Does the headline slant your reading of the story? Explain.	
Story 1:	Story 2:
Briefly describe the factual content of the story. 1. Who is involved? 2. What did he, she, or they do? 3. When did this event happen? 4. Where did it happen? 5. Why did it happen? 6. How did it happen?	
Story 1:	Story 2:
Identify politically charged labels, adjectives, and verbs. For example, is a group called freedom fighters? What term is used to describe those who support abortion rights?	
Story 1:	Story 2:
Now consider how effectively sources (i.e., quotations) were used. 1. Did they add to the credibility of the story? Explain. 2. Did they make the story more interesting? Explain. 3. Did they fairly present differing points of view about the topic? Explain. 4. Are any views missing?	
Story 1:	Story 2:
Compare photographs and photo captions to the news stories connected with them. How does the image affect your understanding of the story?	
Story 1:	Story 2:
Discuss the accuracy of the facts used in the story. How do you know that the sources used were reliable and accurate? Provide specific examples	
Story 1:	Story 2:
How do these stories complement one another? What questions are raised for you? What is left unanswered by these two accounts of this event?	

Lesson 9: Which Source Does the Job?

This lesson gives students an opportunity to pull it all together and apply what they know about news sources to an actual research question.

Model Question

How can equity between urban and suburban school systems in the northeastern United States be reconciled? Why is there such a big achievement gap in education?

Ask students to examine multiple sources from the same news publication about this topic. Be sure that each source is published in a different section of that publication so that the purposes and attributes of each source varies. For example, a search of the *New York Times* on this topic could provide students with:

- An article from the business section on the education gap between rich and poor students (Porter).
- An editorial from the opinion section about the good news surrounding educational inequality (Reardon).
- An entry in the well blog about using meditation to close the achievement gap (Rosenthal).
- Another editorial about why the gap persists ("Why the Achievement Gap Persists").

For each of the sources you curate from a news website, ask students to explain:

- Will this source be useful for answering the model question?
- How you could use the information provided by the source?
- What might make this source valuable for answering this question?
- What issues or questions are raised by this source?
- What other sources do you need to supplement or complement this source?

REFERENCES

Porter, Eduardo. "Education Gap between Rich and Poor Is Growing Wider." *New York Times*, September 22, 2015. http://nytimes.com/2015/09/23/business /economy/education-gap-between-rich-and-poor-is-growing-wider.html.

Reardon, Sean F., Jane Waldfogel, and Daphna Bassok. "The Good News about Educational Equality," *New York Times*, August 26, 2016. http://nytimes.com /2016/08/28/opinion/sunday/the-good-news-about-educational-inequality .html.

Rosenthal, Norman E. "Using Meditation to Help Close the Achievement Gap," *New York Times*, June 2, 2016. https://well.blogs.nytimes.com/2016/06/02/using -meditation-to-help-close-the-achievement-gap.

"Why the Achievement Gap Persists." Editorial. *New York Times*, December 8, 2006. http://nytimes.com/2006/12/08/opinion/08fri1.html.

Lesson 10: How Can Two Writers Reach Such Different Conclusions?

For this exercise, the text selection is key. When doing this exercise with students, be sure to select excerpts from texts that discuss the same content but in different ways. In these examples, students will compare Edmund Morgan's *The Birth of the Republic 1763–89* and Howard Zinn's *A People's History of the United States*. In the selected passages, Morgan and Zinn discuss exactly the same primary sources, yet they arrive at different interpretations of and conclusions about the events and people described in the resources. This comparison compels students to confront their assumptions about historical truth and expand their capacity for understanding disparate points of view.

The American Revolution: Told and Retold

Consider the similarities and differences between these paired passages. In each pair, the first is from Zinn, the second from Morgan. They are describing the same event. As you read, consider these questions about your thinking process:

- What do you choose to believe about the American Revolution? Why?
- Where in these segments do you find yourself saying, "This is not what I thought"?
- How does your *thinking* need to change to embrace more than one, conflicting version of the truth?

And these questions about the people of the Revolutionary era:

- What groups did people join? What motivated membership in and participation in the activities of the associations people joined?
- What notion of liberty did the groups have? How or did group membership influence behavior and belief? Why or why not?
- What impact can/does class, race, and gender have on the waging of sociopolitical revolution and the creation of a new nation? On a person's understanding of liberty?

Stamp Act

When riots against the Stamp Act swept Boston in 1767, they were analyzed by the commander of the British forces in North America, General Thomas Gage, as follows:

The Boston Mob, raised first by the Instigation of Many of the Principal Inhabitants, Allured by Plunder, rose shortly after of their own Accord, attacked, robbed, and destroyed several Houses, and amongst others, that of the Lieutenant Governor. . . . People then began to be terrified at the Spirit they had raised, to perceive that popular Fury was not to be guided, and each individual feared he might be the next Victim to their Rapacity. The same Fears spread thro' the other Provinces, and there has been as much Pains taken since, to prevent Insurrections, of the People, as before to excite them.

Gage's comment suggests that leaders of the movement against the Stamp Act had instigated crowd action but then became frightened by the thought that it might be directed against their wealth too. At this time, the top 10 percent of Boston's taxpayers held about 66 percent of Boston's taxable wealth, while the lowest 30 percent of the taxpaying population had no taxable property at all. The propertyless could not vote and so (like blacks, women, Indians) could not participate in town meetings. This included sailors, journeymen, apprentices, servants (p. 65).

Meanwhile, Bostonians found mobbing so effective a weapon that they used it gratuitously on Lieutenant-Governor Hutchinson, whom they wrongly suspected of advocating the Stamp Act, on the Comptroller of Customs, and on one of the officers of the admiralty court. The other colonies took up the example, and by November 1, 1765, no one in America was prepared to distribute the stamped paper, which was safely stowed away in forts and warships. When that date arrived, there was a pause in business in most colonies as people made up their minds which way to nullify the act by doing nothing that required the use of stamps or by proceeding without them. Once the latter course was chosen by determined groups of citizens, they found it easy, by the mere threat of mob action, to coerce recalcitrant dissenters, including the royally appointed customs officers. Within a few months, the ports were open for business as usual with no sign of a stamp (though, because of the boycott, cargoes from England were few). The courts too were open, and unstamped newspapers appeared weekly, full of messages encouraging the people to stand firm (p. 21).

French Indian (Seven Years') War

After 1763, with England victorious over France in the Seven Years' War (known in America as the French and Indian War), expelling them from North America, ambitious colonial leaders were no longer threatened by the French. They now had only two rivals left: the English and the Indians. The British, wooing the Indians, had declared Indian lands beyond the Appalachians out of bounds to whites (the Proclamation of 1763). Perhaps once the British were out of the way, the Indians could be dealt with. Again, no conscious forethought strategy by the colonial elite, just a growing awareness as events developed.

With the French defeated, the British government could turn its attention to tightening control over the colonies. It needed revenues to pay for the war, and looked to the colonies for that. Also, the colonial trade had become more and more important to the British economy, and more profitable: it had amounted to about 500,000 pounds in 1700 but by 1770 was worth 2,800,000 pounds.

So, the American leadership was less in need of English rule, the English more in need of the colonists' wealth. The elements were there for conflict.

The war had brought glory for the generals, death to the privates, wealth for the merchants, unemployment for the poor. There were 25,000 people living in New York (there had been 7,000 in 1720) when the French and Indian War ended. A newspaper editor wrote about the growing "Number of Beggars and wandering Poor" in the streets of the city. Letters in the papers questioned the distribution of wealth: "How often have our Streets been covered with Thousands of Barrels of Flour for trade, while our near Neighbors can hardly procure enough to make a Dumplin to satisfy hunger?" (p. 59)

No one likes to pay taxes, and the English in 1763 thought they had too many. Though they were the most powerful nation in the world and the most prosperous, their government was costing too much. They had just completed the very expensive Seven Years' War against France, doubling the national debt. The war had also left them with a huge new territory to administer: Canada and the eastern Mississippi valley. Many of them thought the whole of it not worth keeping and when they heard that the government was going to assign ten thousand troops to defend and pacify it, they could only think of how much that many men would eat and drink in a year and how many uniforms they would wear out and how much they would have to be paid (p. 14).

As the streets of Boston came alive with scarlet coats and the people grew familiar with the rhythm of marching feet, it came to Americans everywhere that a dreadful suspicion had been confirmed. They had thought it strange five years before when they heard that England would maintain 10,000 troops among them to protect them from foreign enemies. Hitherto for more than a hundred and fifty years, while hacking out their farms from a hostile wilderness, they had been left to defend themselves, not only against the Indians, but against the French and Spaniards as well. Only in the recent Seven Years' War had they relied heavily on British troops, and those troops had succeeded in removing their gravest peril, the French menace in Canada. Why at precisely this moment, when the danger had departed, should England decide that they needed a standing army to protect them? (p. 43)

REFERENCES

Morgan, Edmund S. *The Birth of the Republic 1763–89.* Chicago: University of Chicago Press, 1977.

Zinn, Howard. *A People's History of the United States.* New York: Harper Perennial Modern Classics, 2005.

Lesson 11: Editorials, Op-Eds, and Blogs, Oh My!

This lesson invites students to examine authorship in editorial writing. So that they don't dismiss a source because of its form, it is important that they learn to dig into authors' backgrounds and make informed judgments about the utility of a source based on that examination rather than its news categorization.

Ask students to compare the two writers from a well-known publication. Be sure that the publication provides a substantial professional biography that is easily accessible to readers. Students can use the keywords that describe bias and types of media from Lesson 8 to explain these writers' jobs. Consider the potential usefulness and hindrances of their writing to any research.

In their online opinion section, the *New York Times* allows readers to select individual columnists and read a collection of that writer's essays. On each writer's page, beneath his or her name, is the beginning of a description of the writer ending with the word "More." Clicking on "More" opens the rest of the description of that columnist; those short biographies are particularly useful for this exercise.

Lesson 12: Reading for Editorial Bias

Once students understand their own information filters, they are better able to recognize the bias of other creators and dispensers of information. As consumption of news and information becomes increasingly digital and less and less on paper, the definition of op-ed may be less necessary than it once was. However, the distinction between op-ed and editorial is still potent and relevant to critical reading.

Organizer for Close Reading of Opinion Writing

Author	Essay Title
Writer's Background Whose opinion is being expressed in this text? Is it an op-ed or an editorial? What is important relevant information to know about the writer before reading the opinion piece?	
Summary of Content What do you think the text is about? What is one line in this text that best summarizes the passage, and what does it mean? What is the topic of the editorial and the opinion of the writer?	
Author's Question What line inquiry guided this writer's investigation?	
Your Questions Questions may be posed in order to elicit more detail, see why an author made certain choices, or clarify anything you do not understand	
Perspectives Who might agree with or be persuaded by this opinion piece? Why? What other views might someone else have? Why?	

From *News Literacy: The Keys to Combating Fake News* by Michelle Luhtala and Jacquelyn Whiting. Santa Barbara, CA: Libraries Unlimited. Copyright © 2018

Lesson 13: Not all Editorials Are Essays

Analyzing a Political Cartoon

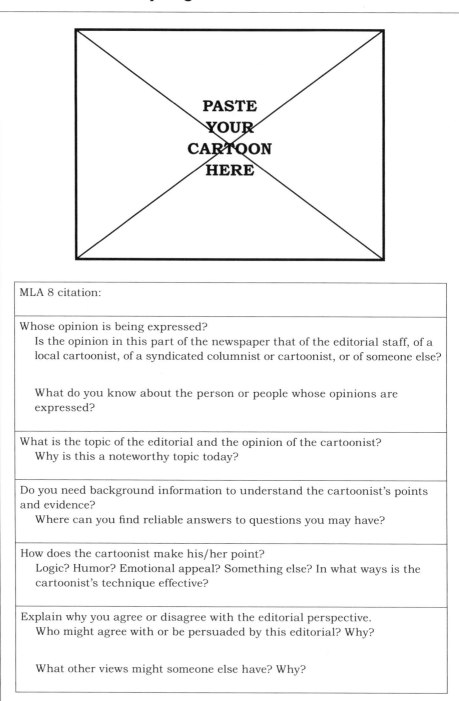

MLA 8 citation:

Whose opinion is being expressed?
    Is the opinion in this part of the newspaper that of the editorial staff, of a
    local cartoonist, of a syndicated columnist or cartoonist, or of someone else?
 	
    What do you know about the person or people whose opinions are
    expressed?

What is the topic of the editorial and the opinion of the cartoonist?   Why is this a noteworthy topic today?
Do you need background information to understand the cartoonist's points and evidence?   Where can you find reliable answers to questions you may have?

How does the cartoonist make his/her point?
    Logic? Humor? Emotional appeal? Something else? In what ways is the
    cartoonist's technique effective?

Explain why you agree or disagree with the editorial perspective.
    Who might agree with or be persuaded by this editorial? Why?
 	
    What other views might someone else have? Why?

From *News Literacy: The Keys to Combating Fake News* by Michelle Luhtala and
Jacquelyn Whiting. Santa Barbara, CA: Libraries Unlimited. Copyright © 2018

Lesson 14: Opinion in Many Forms

The Print Editorial Section vs. The Online One

Students start by examining the first section of a print edition of a newspaper. In the Library Learning Commons (LLC) we have multiple copies of the *New York Times* they can use; we might consider bringing in individual copies of several different newspapers.

The goal is for the students to:

- Locate the Opinion section.
- Discuss why it is located where it is.
- Observe that the page title on the page next to the Opinion page includes the term "**Op-Ed**" (in bold) while other pages do not have special titles.
- Ask questions: what do they want to know about the content of the essays there, the authorship, the editorial selection criteria, the relationships among the writers, their opinions, and the paper.

Next, the students would be directed to examine the digital version of that paper's Opinion section looking for similarities and differences.

- Is different information available online?
- How and why is the presentation format different?
- Which do they prefer? Why?

Incorporate Online Literacy Resources like Newsela

Newsela (http://newsela.com) has an Opinion section in its news collection. They have both opinion essays and PRO/CON comparisons. Each article trailer has icons to give you quick insight into the tools available with that article:

- The lightbulb indicates anchor standards.
- The speech bubble means that suggested text annotations are visible only to the teacher.
- ES means it is also available in Spanish.
- The number **6** means that is the highest grade level for the essay reading level.
- Without a **6**, the articles adjust to grade 12, 10, and 8. The MAX reading level (grade 12) is usually the original text; the lower reading levels are adaptations of the original.
- In this case, the editorial is adapted from what was originally in print rather than being the actual editorial.
- A lightning bolt indicates that "power words" (vocab) are highlighted and defined in the text.

In addition to the opportunities Newsela presents for students to understand bias at an accessible reading level, try asking the students if the adjusted articles maintain the perspective/POV/bias of the original editorial.

Lesson 15: Parody and Satire

If imitation is the truest form of flattery, is imitation that also criticizes the truest insult? For every generation and cultural group, there is pop culture parody. Songs by Weird Al Yankovic and films such as *Airplane: The Movie*, *Spinal Tap*, *Scary Movie*, or *Tropic Thunder* top the list of examples of parody. Each of these examples pokes fun at a popular genre or element of entertainment and does not invite further discourse on an important issue.

Although examples of parody are frequently also called satire, being satirical is more substantive than just poking fun. Through imitation, works that are satirical offer commentary on the nature, audience, context, or message of the original media. Consider this comparison of two recurring sketches on *Saturday Night Live*: the "Jeopardy" spoof and "Mr. Robinson's Neighborhood." In "Jeopardy," Will Ferrell is not offering an opinion about Alex Trebek, the real host of the real *Jeopardy* show. Nor are Darrell Hammond when playing Sean Connery, Molly Shannon as Minnie Driver, or Jimmy Fallon when portraying Hillary Swank. However, when Eddie Murphy plays Mr. Robinson in the satirical sketch series "Mr. Robinson's Neighborhood," commentary on the subject matter and viewership of the children's television show that *Mr. Roger's Neighborhood* is embedded. Understanding that commentary requires viewers to confront their biases about the original program in order to empathize with the worldview being offered by the satire. Without this awareness and commitment by the audience, the "Mr. Robinson's Neighborhood" sketch can only rise to the level of parody. In this way, understanding satire necessitates, at best, that the reader has sophisticated critical reading skills that will serve students well with any text they encounter. At the very least, readers must give themselves permission to question what they are reading or viewing, even if it comes from a source they know and trust. Television programs and films by Jordan Peele and Keegan Michael Key have introduced a new generation of students to the art of satire.

When readers or viewers encounter but do not detect satire, the results are sometimes funny, sometimes alarming. Case in point: the *New York Times* op-ed "College Admissions Shocker!" by Frank Bruni, published on March 30, 2016. In a testament to its exclusivity as an institution of higher learning, Bruni asserted, Stanford University announced a 0 percent acceptance rate for the class of 2020. Bruni claimed to quote a Stanford admissions representative who said, "[W]hile there was a 17-year-old who'd performed surgery, it wasn't open-heart or transplant or anything like that. She'll thrive at Yale." Bruni went on to describe the shockwaves that pervaded the Ivy League and elite college community at the announcement of this news. Those alleged shockwaves were echoed by the real ones that emerged on social media, perpetuated by readers who had not recognized the satire or the reposting of messages by people who never read the original source. One tweeter even suggested that Bruni owed *Times* readers an apology. Remember truthiness? Sometimes your gut might recognize something before your head accepts it.

Try this formula when helping students analyze or create satirical work:

Humor+Informed Criticism=Implicit Argument for Reform

To that end, here are some common devices found in satire. Understanding how these devices can be used to convey an opinion can help students recognize subtleties of meaning and bias in the satire they encounter.

Exaggeration: Hyperbole, caricature, or understatement

Incongruity: Things that are out of place or absurd in relation to their surroundings

Parody: Imitation of techniques or style of some person, place or thing in order to ridicule the original (requires informed audience, who must know the original reference)

Reversal: Presentation of the opposite of the normal order, as in hierarchical order (child runs the family, secretary tells boss how the job is done)

Here are some examples of satire that students can analyze:

- Television: *The Colbert Report*, "Mr. Robinson's Neighborhood" (SNL sketch), Jon Stewart from *The Daily Show* on Teacher Cribs
- Film: *American Psycho*, *The Truman Show*
- Music: "Gangnam Style" by Psy
- Print: *America: Democracy Inaction* by Jon Stewart, *The Sellout* by Paul Beatty
- And the old standby, *The Onion*

Here are some satirical texts students can create:

- Design a travel poster enticing people to live in a medieval village or as the subject of a particular absolutist ruler.
- Retell a text (poem, short story, passage from a novel) as a satirical commentary on the content or context of the original text.
- Write a short story that is a satirical commentary on a particular place and time.
- Interpret a current events issue and convey satirical commentary through a writing or a short video.

REFERENCE

Bruni, Frank. "College Admissions Shocker!" *New York Times*, March 30, 2016. http://nytimes.com/2016/03/30/opinion/college-admissions-shocker.html.

Lesson 16: Propaganda, Hoaxes, and Other Forms of Manipulation

The National Archives and Records Administration offers several guides for helping students unpack primary sources. Inspired by those models, this guide was developed to help students reveal the message in propaganda posters. Furthermore, this guide was created in the context of analyzing World War II propaganda, so it prompts students to compare what they learn about propaganda with their reading of Kurt Vonnegut's *Slaughterhouse-Five*. Completion of this exercise prepares students for interdisciplinary synthesis writing.

Propaganda Analysis Guide

Level 1—OBSERVATION	
Visuals	*Words*
List the objects or people you see in the image	Identify titles, captions, or other written messages
Level 2—INFERENCES	
What symbols do you recognize? Describe any allusions that are being made. What other objects or people work as symbols?	What message is being conveyed by the words? Characterize the message: Is it a warning? An instruction? A compliment? What emotions are being evoked or played upon?
Level 3—TECHNIQUE	

Which of the following techniques apply? (You may check more than one and explain.)

- **Name-Calling:** Linking negative words or phrases with an opposing person, group, or cause to persuade an audience to reject something, based on their emotional response to words rather than on careful consideration of facts
- **Glittering Generalities:** Linking positive, general, and commonly accepted words ("love," "family," "democracy") with a person, group, or cause to make an audience approve without careful consideration
- **Euphemisms:** Substituting words or phrases with softer, more palatable ones to generate a more positive response or to mislead intentionally ("senior citizen" for "old person," "collateral damage" for "civilian casualties")
- **Transfer:** Connecting the authority or prestige of certain images or symbols (the American flag, the cross, science, medicine) with a person or product
- **Testimonial:** Using well-known personalities to endorse a person, group, or cause whether they are experts on the subject or not
- **Plain Folks:** Trying to convince an audience that someone is "one of them"—a common, ordinary, hard-working, all-American citizen instead of a wealthy politician, for example
- **Bandwagon:** Claiming that an audience should do something because "everybody else is doing it"
- **Fear:** Warning an audience that something horrible will happen to them if they don't take a certain action

How do the images and words work together?	
Who was the intended audience for this message? How do you know?	What makes this visual an effective means of delivering the intended message to that group?
Level 4—TEXT CONNECTION	

Where have you encountered propaganda in *literature*? How does it compare with visual propaganda?

Where do you encounter propaganda in *Slaughterhouse-Five* (quote, page numbers)? Is *Slaughterhouse-Five* propaganda? Is Professor Rumfoord's book?

Level 5—CONNECTION	
What is propaganda? When does a persuasive piece become propaganda?	It is not a thing of the past. Identify propaganda to which you are subject and explore the experience of being a recipient of the message.

From *News Literacy: The Keys to Combating Fake News* by Michelle Luhtala and Jacquelyn Whiting. Santa Barbara, CA: Libraries Unlimited. Copyright © 2018

REFERENCE

National Archives and Records Administration. "Document Analysis Worksheets." *Teacher Resources*. United States Government. Accessed May 18, 2017. http://www.archives.gov/education/lessons/worksheets.

Lesson 17: Analysis of Social Media as a Tool for Persuasion

Just as reading and writing are two sides of the same coin, so are detecting tools of persuasion and persuasion itself. Teaching students to recognize ethos, pathos, and logos expands their repertoire of tools for argument—argument, that is, in the Aristotelian sense: civil discourse. A couple of sources deserve a shout-out for inspiring ways to teach students to analyze the information they encounter in social media.

This first of these sources is Anne Kornblut of *The Washington Post*. During a 2012 interview with Steve Inskeep on NPR, she used the phrase "Twitter is the new bus," a statement educators should take to heart when helping students develop news literacy. Inskeep interviewed three reporters on the 2012 campaign trail about a 40-year-old book by Timothy Crouse about the 1972 Nixon-McGovern campaign called *Boys on the Bus*. Here is a segment of their conversation:

Steve Inskeep: "There's another thing that strikes me about this book, and it's the way that there were a few reporters who are identified who seem to influence other reporters. In 1972, I think I think the leading guy was R.W. Apple—Johnny Apple of the *New York Times*."

Jonathan Martin of *Politico*: "Walter Mears too of the AP. There was a saying about, 'What's the lead, Walter?' which was sort of the stock phrase these guys would say on the campaign trail—and that was to Walter Mears, 'What is the news out of this event?' 'What's the lead of the story?' I think that there are still those individuals on the campaign trail, certainly. I think there is much more fragmentation now in the political news media and there are just so many outlets that you don't quite have the same pack journalism that you probably did back in 1972."

Steve Inskeep: "Oh wait a minute, let me just challenge that and you guys tell me if I am wrong. I think if I follow the coverage there are many, many outlets who all will obsess over the same irrelevant story at the same time."

Jonathan Martin: "Oh that's fair. Oh sure."

Ashley Parker of the *New York Times*: "But that's less of turning to one person who's sort of the pack leader and I think part of that is a result of Twitter. Which is that anyone with a handle can Tweet out a story and generate buzz for a story so it doesn't matter if you're the senior correspondent or you're a blog with a scoop. And then it all sort of gets retweeted."

Steve Inskeep: "If you see lots and lots of Tweets about something, do you feel compelled to jump on that story?"

Anne Kornblut: "I think we at least feel compelled to look into it, if nothing else. In a way, Twitter is the new bus." (Boys on the Bus)

Even now, five years later, this piece can still inform planning and pedagogy surrounding news literacy. You may have heard one of the authors (Michelle) mention it during edWeb.net Emerging Tech webinar #74 on media literacy, when she asked *USA Today*'s National K–12 Education Writer Greg Toppo about Ms. Kornblut's comment. He agreed that it was *a* bus but maybe not *the* bus.

Another source of inspiring tools for engaging students in explorations of social media and news literacy is Teach Argument. They do not give everything away for free, but from their free materials you can get a sense of the quality of the lessons they offer. In particular, they suggest directing students to apply well-known tools of rhetorical persuasion to their analysis of media posts:

Ethos appeals to a sense of right and wrong or what is just.
Pathos is an emotional appeal.
Logos uses reason to persuade.

To that end, select a Facebook post that is relevant to your unit or content and relevant tweets. Or tweets that will serve as a good model if you don't want to apply your thinking to the content with which the students will be wrestling. Annotate the posts, highlighting for your students where and how different tools of persuasion are used. Then ask them to apply these skills to a content-related exercise like this one:

In this exercise, students will unpack and analyze twitter hashtags that address potent issues in education and education reform and then create their social media campaign.

Students can work in groups with each group focusing on one of the following hashtag (#) categories. First, review recent posts made using those hashtags.

Gaps	Policy
#achievementgap: Follow this hashtag to learn more about the achievement gap and what activists across the education profession (including parents) have to say about closing it and establishing more opportunities for students caught in the middle.	#edpolicy: perhaps obviously, this hashtag is dedicated to furthering the discussion of current education politics and what needs changing to ensure the best possible environments for kid and adult students alike.
#edgap: Like #achievementgap, #edgap is all about promoting equal opportunities in education, particularly along class, race, gender, and ability lines.	#edpolitics: Politics and education merge in a fireball of . . . well . . . just go give it a read; #edpolitics informs and no doubt nurtures some interesting conversations and debates.
People	**Reform**
#putkidsfirst: Used primarily in Louisiana, #putkidsfirst is a national discussion about budgets, vouchers, and other hot education topics.	#edreform: This hashtag indexes a frequently updated discussion about education reform, featuring a wide spectrum of ideas, insights, and opinions.
#teacherquality: Because teachers stand at the forefront of education, drawing up policies to ensure the best possible output greatly benefits students.	#schoolreform: This is another active, ongoing discussion about changing education at different levels to provide the best possible learning experiences.

Demographics	Statistics
#blackedu: This conversation focuses on in-class strategies and out-of-class policies both negatively and positively impacting black students, with some excellent insight provided by a nice range of participants.	#eddata: Get to number crunching with #eddata and its long-running exchange of statistics relevant to the education industry; compelling research is essential to drawing up the most effective, valuable reformation possible.
#latinoedu: Parents, policy makers, and, of course, education professionals might want to give this Twitter talk a follow when wanting to learn more about providing opportunities for Latino students.	
#nativeedu: The National Indian Education Association primarily uses the quite new #nativeedu to raise awareness of the good and bad policies directly affecting Native American students.	
#urbaned: The hashtag concerns itself with drawing up policies to improve education problems unique to urban and inner-city schools.	

After reviewing the hashtags, each group should identify one *really potent* tweet to analyze, take a screenshot, and paste it into a document where they can annotate it. For example, the following outline can be recreated as a Google Doc and shared with students:

Remember: If the tweet includes an *image*, how does that image advance the message?

Speaker:	Audience:	Message:
Ethos (right and wrong):	Pathos (emotion):	Logos (evidence):
Synthesize (Tweet Purpose):		

Once the students have completed their tweet analysis, it is time to JigSaw: re-form groups so that each group has one person from each of the original groups. Students then share their analysis and collaborate to synthesize the tweets.

Compare and contrast how each of these tweets uses ethos, pathos, and logos. From a rhetorical standpoint, which of these tweets do you consider most effective? Why?
How do the purposes of each of these tweets vary, and how is that reflected in their composition? How are different individuals invested in the same subject matter? How do they choose to approach these "investments"?
How are the purposes of each of your selected tweets similar or different—and *why* are these purposes similar or different? Is it the speaker's choice? Is the speaker somehow restricted?
How does social media advance the discourse happening here? How is it hindered?

No lesson on hashtags would be complete without tweeting!

Direct students to open a Google Slide or some other program for creating an image with text. Direct students to capture their group's big takeaway and add a relevant image that they have permission to use. Download the slide as a jpg so that you can add it to a tweet.

Ask students to tweet out their insight using a class or school account. Be sure to include the school's hashtag or handle.

REFERENCES

"'Boys on the Bus': 40 Years Later, Many Are Girls." Transcript. National Public Radio. April 12, 2012. http://npr.org/templates/transcript/transcript.php ?storyId=150577036.

"Lesson Plans." *Teach Argument.* Accessed May 18, 2017. http://teachargument.com /products.

Lesson 18: Fact-Checkers

Spots, Gulfs, and Politicians Who Lie

Abraham Lincoln established himself on the national political stage with his so-called Spot Resolutions, a series of resolutions he introduced into the House of Representatives in 1847 demanding to know the precise location of the start of the Mexican War. Lincoln was asserting that then President James K. Polk was responsible for provoking skirmishes on Mexican land in order to have an excuse to go war.

Assuming the office of the presidency in 1963 after the assassination of John F. Kennedy, Lyndon B. Johnson inherited responsibility for the international dispute that continued to simmer between the United States and Vietnam. On August 2, 1964. U.S. ships in the Gulf of Tonkin took fire from the North Vietnamese. What happened on August 4 in the Gulf has, for decades, been unclear, but Johnson reported to Congress that "renewed hostile actions against United States ships on the high seas in the Gulf of Tonkin" necessitated a military response, resulting in the Gulf of Tonkin Resolution, which gave the president authority to wage war in Vietnam. For decades, the facts about what happened in the Gulf of Tonkin in the first week of August 1964 have been debated. The release of previously classified documents in 2005 and 2006 point to intentional deceit by Defense Secretary Robert McNamara, which contributed to the confusion on August 4 when an alleged attack on U.S. ships occurred.

President George W. Bush sought permission to invade Iraq to find and destroy the weapons of mass destruction his administration insisted were there. As with the Gulf of Tonkin, Congress responded with military authorization. Weapons of mass destruction were never found in Iraq.

So we have a loose pattern of allegations against presidents and their security advisors of intentionally misleading the public to gain support for war. These allegations originate not from conspiracy theorists spouting wild accusations but from truth seekers concerned that wars were being fought and people were dying for fabricated reasons. Because someone lied. Why are we so willing to believe that political figures lie to us? Easy: because sometimes they do.

Case in point: Gary Hart. The former senator, when he was seeking the democratic nomination to run for president, was accused of having an extramarital affair. Hart responded by taunting the press and getting caught. Hart was quoted by the *New York Times* magazine as saying: "Follow me around. . . . I'm serious. If anybody wants to put a tail on me, go ahead. They'd be very bored." Reporters did just what he asked, and within days his candidacy ended when his affair was exposed.

We and our students can't follow elected leaders or candidates around all day waiting to see whether they are truthful, so we turn to investigative journalists to be our fact-checkers. Teaching students the habits of mind and protocols of being a fact-checker could be an interesting part of their digital literacy in this age when not all that appears to be investigative news reporting actually is.

The Lesson Plan: Teaching Students to Be Fact-Checkers

Here are the websites for four organizations whose mission is to fact-check stories that are circulated in popular media or asserted by politicians.

- Snopes: http://www.snopes.com
- FactCheck.org: http://factcheck.org
- Politifact: http://www.politifact.com
- *The Washington Post* Fact Checker: https://www.washingtonpost.com /news/fact-checker

They all have an About Us section in which they explain who they are, their founding mission, and the processes they use to evaluate assertions. All four accept questions from the public about issues to be examined. All explain how their sites are funded. They assert their shared belief in transparency.

Group students, and ask each group to examine the processes used by one of the fact-checkers. Then jigsaw the groups and have them compare the protocols used by the different organizations.

Each group should then create a "best of" set of protocols, drawing from the four different organizations and devising a rating system for evaluating "truthiness."

Working as a team, they apply these protocols to an assertion made in the media. Perhaps each group is given a tweet or Facebook post by a politician to fact-check. Perhaps they listen to an interview with a political figure and evaluate the assertions made during that interview.

The groups then rate the truthfulness of their source and share with the class, explaining how they arrived at their rating.

If students are in the process of researching, considering having them do this exercise with the sources they are finding (ideas adapted from Valenza):

Divide the class into six groups. Assign each group one of the following prompts to discuss, then share out their conclusions with the class.

Group 1: News used to be delivered once a day for an hour on television or in the morning newspaper. Now we have a 24/7 news cycle, where news is constantly breaking. Why does this matter?

Group 2: We used to get news from weekly magazines, daily newspapers, or nightly news broadcasts via television or radio. Now news streams across media platforms and devices. Why does this matter?

Group 3: We used to trust investigative journalists to expose hoaxes. Now people can pretend to be journalists and perpetrate the hoaxes. Why does this matter?

Group 4: Journalism used to be a profession that required specific training in both writing and ethics. Now citizen-journalists can generate content from anywhere and anytime. Why does this matter?

Group 5: We used to have to actively change the channel (or buy another newspaper) to filter the information we received. Now our social media likes create "echo chambers," and we might not even realize these filters exist. Why does this matter?

Group 6: News companies, large and small, have always had owners. Today, very few small news companies remain because a few wealthy owners have created information monopolies. Why does this matter?

After they share, direct them to consider one of the sources they are using for their research and to answer each of the following questions about that source:

- What version of the story did you access? Has it changed since you accessed it? If so, how? If someone accessed it earlier than you, does that person's understanding of the issue differ from yours?
- In what media form did your source reach you (TV, radio, YouTube, blog, etc.)? How does the format impact the information it contains?
- What is the URL of your source location? What information about the source does the URL provide?
- Who is the author, and what is that person's expertise with regard to the topic of the source?
- On a scale of 1–10 (1 is never, 10 is all the time), how often do you consult this source for information?
- Who owns the publication you consulted? And, considering also your answer to the previous question, how might that influence the information you know?

REFERENCE

Valenza, Joyce. "Truth, Truthiness, Triangulation: A News Literacy Toolkit for a "Post-Truth World." *NeverEnding Search*. November 26, 2016. http://blogs.slj .com/neverendingsearch/2016/11/26/truth-truthiness-triangulation-and -the-librarian-way-a-news-literacy-toolkit-for-a-post-truth-world/.

Lesson 19: Anatomy of a Stump Speech

During the run-up to the party conventions for the 2012 presidential election, the *New York Times* published an online interactive titled "Anatomy of a Stump Speech" (http://www.nytimes.com/interactive/2012/01/03/us/politics /gop-stump-speeches.html). In their annotations on four different speeches, *The Times* reporters examined the rhetorical devices being used, looked at the common elements of such speeches, and also provided fact-checking of the candidates' assertions.

Here are some suggestions for how to incorporate this interactive resource in class.

- Divide students into groups. Assign each group one of the elements of a stump speech: home field advantage and local color, staying positive, use of catch phrases, themes important to the party, attacks on the opponent, and the like. Ask students to compare and contrast how different candidates' speeches use the device and which they find most effective.
- Next, provide students an unannotated speech and ask them to analyze the new speech looking for use of these key elements.
- Finally, students can write a speech for a favorite candidate or write the speech by which they would be most convinced to support a candidate, among other possibilities.

Each of these exercises is asking students to consider the subtleties of word usage (connotation and denotation), as well as the context in which arguments are made. Both are critical elements of savvy information literacy.

Lesson 20: Unpacking a Visual Text—Paintings

Analyzing paintings—any works of art, really—requires that students keep in mind the relationships between the artist and the subject and between the artist and the painting. Students must remember that every element of a painting is the conscious choice of the artist: every color, gesture, expression, brush stroke, object, and so on. And your students may challenge you and sometimes say that things just happen when an artist is making a painting, but if it remains when the painting is complete, then its inclusion was still a conscious choice. The following organizer guides students in examining each of these relationships and the artist's choices in order to extract meaning from a work of art.

Making Meaning of a Visual Text

List *what* <u>you</u> *see*: Make no evaluations or judgments. For example, don't say, "I see a poor person." "Poor" is a judgment. What do you see that leads you to that judgment?

Questions of the Artist	Questions of the Subject(s)	Questions of History
1.	1.	1.
2.	2.	2.
3.	3.	3.
4.	4.	4.

<u>Inferences</u>: Consider message and meaning by synthesizing answers to your questions with the elements of the image.

Each person in your group should choose a different person in the painting to consider; for your person, answer the following questions, then share as a group:

What can this person see?
What might this person know, understand, or believe?
About what might this person care deeply?
What might this person wonder or question?
What makes this painting work?

Consider using images like *Daniel Boone Escorting Settlers through the Cumberland Gap* (1851–1852) by George Caleb Bingham, and ask students to apply the artist's message to the concept of the Social Contract. Or select *An Experiment on a Bird in an Air Pump* (1768) by Joseph Wright of Derby, and ask students to consider how the painting is connected to the Enlightenment.

From *News Literacy: The Keys to Combating Fake News* by Michelle Luhtala and Jacquelyn Whiting. Santa Barbara, CA: Libraries Unlimited. Copyright © 2018

Lesson 21: Unpacking a Visual Text—Photographs

Just as everything in a painting is the conscious choice of the artist, so, too, students must learn to approach photographs with a similar mind to question the photographer's purpose and meaning. In fact, the proliferation of handheld digital devices has made virtually every person a photographer. Photography is no longer a craft relegated to artists, nor is a photographer limited by exposures on rolls of film and the time necessary to chemically process it. Snapchatting, Instagram-posting students need to learn to be skeptical consumers of photographic record and not assume that all photos were candidly created and that they capture a moment in time. Photographs can be as composed and posed as paintings or taken in series, with only one of the images gaining iconic status, as is the case with the exercise here. Please visit the Library of Congress website for access to each of the photographs referenced in this exercise (http://loc.gov/rr/print/list/128_migm.html).

In 1936 in California, photographer Dorothea Lange photographed a destitute migrant mother. (See Figure 6.3.)

Destitute Pea Pickers, also known as Migrant Mother, by Dorothea Lange

Photograph	Lange's Negative Descriptions	Lange's Recollections
FIGURE 6.3A Destitute Pea Pickers. Library of Congress, Prints & Photographs Division, FSA/OWI Collection, [LC-USF34-9095].	"Destitute peapickers in California; a 32 year old mother of seven children. February 1936" (retouched version).	"I saw and approached the hungry and desperate mother, as if drawn by a magnet. I do not remember how I explained my presence or my camera to her, but I do remember she asked me no questions. I made five exposures, working closer and closer from the same direction. I did not ask her name or her history. She told me her age, that she was thirty-two. She said that they had been living on frozen vegetables from the surrounding fields, and birds that the children killed. She had just sold the tires from her car to buy food. There she sat in that lean-to tent with her children huddled around her, and seemed to know that my pictures might help her, and so she helped me. There was a sort of equality about it." (From: *Popular Photography*, Feb. 1960).
FIGURE 6.3B Destitute Pea Pickers. Library of Congress, Prints & Photographs Division, FSA/OWI Collection, [LC-USF34-9093-C].	"Migrant agricultural worker's family. Seven children without food. Mother aged 32, father is a native Californian. March 1936."	
FIGURE 6.3C Destitute Pea Pickers. Library of Congress, Prints & Photographs Division, FSA/OWI Collection, [LC-USF34-9097-C].	"Nipomo, Calif. Mar. 1936. Migrant agricultural worker's family. Seven hungry children. Mother aged 32, the father is a native Californian. Destitute in a pea pickers camp, because of the failure of the early pea crop. These people had just sold their tent in order to buy food. Most of the 2,500 people in this camp were destitute."	
FIGURE 6.3D Destitute Pea Pickers. Library of Congress, Prints & Photographs Division, FSA/OWI Collection, [LC-USZ62-58355].	"Nipomo, Calif. Mar. 1936. Migrant agricultural worker's family. Seven hungry children. Mother aged 32. Father is a native Californian."	

From *News Literacy: The Keys to Combating Fake News* by Michelle Luhtala and Jacquelyn Whiting. Santa Barbara, CA: Libraries Unlimited. Copyright © 2018

Students can use the same methodology that was applied to the painting in order to unpack the photograph. Then they can apply the following ideas to interpreting Lange's work and purpose:

Message: What is being said?

Method: How is it said—the composition?

Medium: What materials and channels of communication (i.e., the media) are used?

Audience: For whom is the text composed? Who is the intended recipient of the message?

Purpose: What is the overall goal, aim, or intended effect—the agenda or response it intends to elicit?

Context: What immediately surrounds the text, the historical, social, or economic environment?

FIGURE 6.3 Migrant Mother. Library of Congress, Prints & Photographs Division, FSA/OWI Collection, [LC-USF34-009058-C].

Is the text meant for a particular context? Is it a work of art? A commercial piece? Some combination of the two? Something else entirely? How does composition (line, color, arrangement) convey emotion or symbolism? Is the subject matter abstract or representational? What is the relationship between the idea being represented and the subjects used in the representation?

REFERENCES

Atwan, Robert. *Convergences: Message, Method, Medium.* 2nd ed. New York: St. Martin's Press, 2004.

"Dorothea Lange's 'Migrant Mother' Photographs in the Farm Security Administration Collection: An Overview." Compiled by Prints and Photography Division, Library of Congress. 2004. http://www.loc.gov/rr/print/list/128_migm.html.

Lesson 22: Building Capacities for Critical Thinking by Fostering Empathy

Empathy is one of the most important skills for digital natives to develop. Certainly empathy is a key element in accessing "Migrant Mother's" expression. The ease with which our students navigate social media and potentially establish global connections necessitates that they learn to understand the perspectives of people quite different from themselves. Sam Richards, in his TED Talk, "A Radical Experiment in Empathy," does an excellent job of guiding his audience to understand what empathy is and why it matters that students and adults develop this capacity. It is incumbent upon us as educators to design exercises that challenge students to explore many different points of view, both historical and current.

Consider beginning units with an "empathy challenge." Ask your students to anticipate how what they are about to study will be difficult for them to understand? How will they try to understand the people who hold these unfamiliar or even offensive views? Developing empathy can also be the goal of an exercise, such as the following one.

Practice Empathy with History

What Are the Ripple Effects of My Decisions?

Step 1: Choose a perspective.

- William Lloyd Garrison
- Frederick Douglass
- John C. Calhoun
- A slave (Consider narratives such as Rose Williams'.)
- Sojourner Truth
- John Brown
- Nat Turner
- Harriet Tubman

Step 2: Walk the plantation.

- Pass the fields where the slaves are picking cotton, the mule-driven cotton gin, the extended family at the quarters, and the punished slave on your way to the manor house.
- Make observations? What did you see? Hear?

For this exercise, provide students with images to reference. Set up the images as a gallery walk. The Mississippi Department of Archives and History is a good source of photographs of slaves working in the fields and of 19th-century cotton gin operations. Many public domain images are available online of slaves in their quarters and working in fields, as well as plantation manor houses. The iconic image of the slave, "Scourged Black," is also fitting for this exercise. (An image search for the keywords slave "Peter scars" will return many images that can be used in class; in addition, this image is available in many U.S. history textbooks.)

Step 3: At each viewing point, make a decision.

- Remembering which perspective you chose, what would you do? Why?
- Consider the following motives. Which is most appropriate for your person? Why? How ethical is your person?
  1. **Golden Rule**: "How would I like it if someone did it to me?" Or "Do unto others as you would have others do unto you."
  2. **Rule of Accepted Principles of Ethical Conduct**: "Is it allowed by the Ten Commandments or the Six Pillars of Character?"
  3. **Rule of Universality**: "How would it be if everyone did it?"
  4. **Rule of Disclosure**: "How would I feel if the whole world knew what I was doing or going to do, especially my family and school or business associates?"
  5. **Rule of the Most Honoring Choice**: When there is a conflict between our own values or between our values and those of others affected by the decision, we should then choose the alternative that honors the most important long-term values for those most affected. Balance the possible good against the possible harm while serving those to whom you have an obligation.
  6. **Rule of the Ends Justify the Means**: If it's necessary, then it's ethical, no matter how it gets done.
  7. **Rule of Law**: If it's legal and permissible, it's proper and ethical.
  8. **Rule of Business, Nothing Personal**: It's just part of the job, so I can or must do it.
  9. **Rule of the Good Cause**: Sometimes people get hurt in the name of a good cause.
  10. **Rule of Other**: "I was just doing it for you."
  11. **Rule of Reciprocity**: "I'm just fighting fire with fire."
  12. **Rule of No Harm, No Foul**: "It doesn't hurt anyone, so why shouldn't I do it?"
  13. **Rule of No Exception**: "Everyone's doing it, so I should too?"
  14. **Rule of Selflessness**: "It's OK if I don't gain personally."
  15. **Rule of Earned Reward**: "I deserve it."
  16. **Rule of Just Desserts**: "She's/he's got it coming."

Another approach to building empathy is by subtly embedding it in mentor texts you use. Many educators have embraced the This I Believe program begun in 1951 by Edward R. Murrow when Murrow, a preeminent journalist, decided that the American public lacked necessary empathy for progress as a global leader. His hope was that, by providing a forum for people of all different walks of life to share snippets of their life philosophy, we would learn to appreciate the strength of diversity in society. The essays written for this program can serve as excellent models for personal essays. A favorite is "Be Cool to the Pizza Dude" by Sarah Adams. When National Public Radio aired Adams reading her essay they introduced her by saying, "Sarah Adams has held many jobs in her life, including telemarketer, factory worker, hotel clerk and flower shop cashier, but has never delivered pizzas." This biographical description underscores Adams's entreaty that we act with humility and grace and engage one another with empathy and respect).

A component of critical reading and source evaluation is an open mind. Search engine and social media algorithms filter the information we receive so that we are fed what reinforces our prior searches and points of view, and sources that are contrary to our views don't reach us. Students need to be encouraged to seek sources that challenge their beliefs, assumptions, and worldview in order to be global citizens and valuable contributors to civil discourse.

Joining the Conversation

Ultimately, the goal of educators is to have students create their own media to communicate their learning with an audience beyond their teacher or their classroom. These lessons allow students to apply what they learned in earlier lessons in terms of critical source review and analysis in order to create and distribute products of their research.

REFERENCES

Adams, Sarah. "Be Cool to the Pizza Dude." *This I Believe.* May 16, 2005. http://thisibelieve.org/essay/23. https://www.npr.org/2005/05/16/4651531/be-cool-to-the-pizza-dude.

Richards, Sam. "A Radical Experiment in Empathy." TED video, 18:07. October 2012. http://ted.com/talks/sam_richards_a_radical_experiment_in_empathy.

Lesson 23: Branding and Advertising

This lesson idea is inspired by *Harper's Magazine* writer Thomas Frank, who wrote:

> One of the criticisms of Washington that you hear all the time is that if only the federal government was run more like a business, then it wouldn't be so awful and so dreadful. Well, we thought about it. One of the things that the federal government would do if it was run by, like a business, is it would advertise. It wouldn't let its brand get run down in the way that—I mean, the federal government is uniquely unpopular.

Franks' assessment of the government's image problem led *Harper's* to a unique proposition. As described in an NPR story, *Harper's Magazine* challenged four advertising agencies to create Super Bowl commercials that would rebrand the American government ("Imagine This"). While these agencies engaged in the intellectual exercise posed by this challenge, they did not actually create the ads, but students could accept this challenge and make the Super Bowl commercials to sell the government back to the American people.

First, the students have to learn that branding is really selling a *promise* more than a *product*. Branding sells power, identity, purpose.

To that end, invite students to examine a familiar print ad such as the Nike "swoosh" with their slogan: "Just Do It." Guide students' examination and discussion of this ad campaign with questions like these:

- What do you think about this image?
- How does it make you feel?
- What associations do you have with it?
- What is "*it*"?

See how many different responses there are when students try to define "it," and ask them to discuss why that range of answers matters in this ad campaign.

Next, to understand how television commercials work, invite your students to watch the series of Mac commercials that featured Justin Long as Mac and John Hodgman as PC, and then discuss what they see with these suggested questions as a guide.

Content
- Who is the audience?
- What behavior is the ad trying to prompt? (What do they want the viewer to do?)
- What attitude are they trying to change or create? (What do they want the viewer to believe?)
- What do they want the viewer to repeat to other people (the tag line)?
- What is the overall message?

Visual Elements

- Is the setting always the same? If so, why? If it changes, why does it change?
- The color scheme: how does it work?
- The spokesperson: does the viewer like him/her? Why or why not?

So far, these ads have sold both an image and product. Now consider ads that rebrand something. In other words, branding features ads that are trying to change or improve an image. Two possible re-branding ads to consider come from the Chrysler campaign to remake the image of Detroit, Michigan. Both feature Eminem as a spokesperson. The commercials are viewable on Chrysler's YouTube channel ("Chrysler Eminem"). View the commercials twice. The first time, just watch. The second time, present the following questions first and ask the students to make notes in response to them while and after they watch and listen:

- Who is the audience?
- What attitude is being changed or created? (What do they want the viewer to believe?)
- Who is the spokesperson? What impact does he/she have on the message? Does the ad work even if the viewer doesn't recognize the spokesperson? Explain.
- How does the soundtrack work? How does it work with the spokesperson?
- What is the overall message?

Now students are ready to become creators of a re-branding campaign. You could use the premise that inspired *Harper's* and ask students to rebrand the U.S. government and sell it back to the American people, or you could substitute an image problem relevant to your learning community, and the students could work to solve the local problem.

The prompts that follow use rebranding the government as the subject of the exercise, and you can modify them to address the topic of focus that you or your students identity. Either way, first the students have to make some decisions:

- What is it about the government that needs rebranding?
- What attributes have people forgotten?
- Why is the U.S. system better than other types of governments?
- What benefits can people get from this system and not from others?
- What is the price of losing this government?

Students can work collaboratively to compile audio, video, text, and still image resources. Remind them that in the sample ads they reviewed, every aspect from color to voice-over to camera angle to music was carefully designed and selected for maximum rebranding impact. Nothing was included by accident. Before the students begin filming or composing their ad, they need a plan, storyboard, or treatment in which the student teams provide the following information about their ads:

- What is the main goal and focus of this spot?
- Who is your audience?
- Will you use humor? Horror? Tug heart strings? Hit with facts?
- Explain why—what thoughts or emotion will each ad evoke from your audience?
- Will you use metaphor? Symbols? To what end? What will they make your audience think or feel?
- Will there be music? What kind? What effect will it have on your audience?
- What will the visuals be? Still images (photos, posters, graphics, paintings)? Moving footage? In color or black and white? Sepia? Posterized? What will the effect be on the audience?
- Will you use actors? What type of characters will they play? What will they say? Do? How will the audience react?
- Who isn't going to like what you are doing? Is there a way to get those people to buy into your message? Is it worth changing your plan to capture any audience that might be put off by your approach?
- What commercial or movie scene are you picturing in your head that you are trying to make your scene resemble?

Summation

We, the ad makers, are going to do [*this*] so the viewer feels [*this*].

Now they are ready to film! (See a suggested rubric for this exercise in Chapter 10.)

REFERENCES

"Chrysler Eminem Super Bowl Commercial—Imported From Detroit." Posted by Chrysler. February 5, 2011. YouTube video, 2:02. http://www.youtube.com/watch?v=SKL254Y_jtc.

"Imagine This: A Super Bowl Ad for the Government." Transcript. All Things Considered. National Public Radio. February 4, 2011. Accessed January 10, 2017. http://npr.org/2011/02/04/133504071/Imagine-This-A-Super-Bowl-Ad-For-The-Government.

Lesson 24: Expose the Trail

Similar to the work of Bergstrom and West at the University of Washington, journalist and Pace University Professor Andy Revkin created an exercise for his graduate students:

A "Backtrack Journal" is a standing assignment. This is the task:

Each week, determine the path one bit of information took to get to you. If it was a powerful photo of a drowned refugee child, did it come via Facebook? Twitter? If so, was it forwarded by a friend from some other friend or feed? Who created the content? Try to trace how information MOVES (Revkin).

Here is an adaptation for students younger than college age. This lesson is a good complement to the lesson on analyzing the ethos, pathos, and logos of a tweet!

Finding the Horse's Mouth

Screenshot or copy-and-paste the original social media post here:

Add the MLA 8 citation:

Identify the sender or poster of the message.	Is it a person, company, organization or something else?
Can you find a website?	Paste URL here: Read "About Us" section; explain their expertise on this topic.

If there is a website without any information about the creator, is the website suspicious for any reason?

If there is no website, what else can you find out about the author of the post? How reliable does she/he seem? Why?

Create a new social media post that explains the credibility of the original post (or lack thereof) that can be posted to social media to help your friends and followers unpack the information they receive. You can use words, images, a snapshot of the original post, weblinks, and annotations to convey your message. Paste a screenshot of your post here:

From *News Literacy: The Keys to Combating Fake News* by Michelle Luhtala and Jacquelyn Whiting. Santa Barbara, CA: Libraries Unlimited. Copyright © 2018

REFERENCE

Revkin, Andy. "Tools and Techniques for Tracking How #FakeNews (or the Real Thing) Flows". August 23, 2016. http://medium.com/@revkin/to-see-how-information-flows-online-try-a-backtrack-journal-e5e65e56bf6c.

Lesson 25: Protection by the First Amendment

The *New York Times* Learning Network has an interesting exercise for students about press censorship in which they suggest that students skim issues of the *New York Times* and pick out articles or images that they think or feel would probably not be published in a country without a guarantee of freedom of the press ("Censoring the Press"). This is a rich exercise that can inspire interesting and thoughtful class discussion. Here is our corollary to the *Times* suggestion:

Tank Man and Other Fake News

(Due to copyright protections, the image of "tank man" could not be reproduced here; however, teachers can find this image digitally and project it for students to examine.)	Do you recognize this image? What do you notice? What do you know about this image? How do you know all that you do?
Why would this image and the corresponding video footage not be aired in China or available via the Internet in China?	
Find another image that you know or suspect would not be published in a country where the media is censored by the government; paste it here with the MLA 8 citation:	Explain why you selected this image, what you know about the situation it depicts, and what you think the value of this image is to the people of the country where it was taken and/or to the global community.

From *News Literacy: The Keys to Combating Fake News* by Michelle Luhtala and Jacquelyn Whiting. Santa Barbara, CA: Libraries Unlimited. Copyright © 2018

Exercises like this encourage students to consider the role of the free press in democratic society. A primary role of the U.S. Supreme Court is to balance the rights of the individuals with the needs and expectations of the common good as measured against the provisions of the U.S. Constitution. A free press, as outlined in the First Amendment, is intended to protect both the rights of the publisher of the press and the right of the people to know. As teachers and school librarians teach students to examine their sources of information and develop news literacy, they must reinforce that it is the privilege of maintaining a healthy and robust First Amendment that obligates them to this charge.

REFERENCE

"Censoring the Press." Learning Network. *New York Times*. Accessed May 18, 2017. http://static01.nyt.com/images/blogs/learning/pdf/activities/Censoring Press_NYTLN.pdf.

Lesson 26: Media Watch

In this mini unit, students apply their critical reading and viewing skills to mainstream media and join the conversation. The essential question, "How do your sources of information affect how you view the world around you?"

Phase I

Your job is to choose a current events issue and track it in the media for the next few weeks.

* You should consult *at least* **two** sources *at least* **three** times each week.
* Keep a journal in which you log your considerations by date and time.

Here are suggestions for how to approach the journal:

* A Google Doc works well for this project.
* If you would like to work with a partner (see the point–counterpoint nature of Challenge Option 1 in the Phase II section), you could create your own Google Site or Blog on which you document your considerations publicly.

Consider these below to guide your reflection:

* What do you think the issue is about?
* From where did you gain this understanding?
* In what ways do the following sources offer similar coverage of the issue? Be specific; quote and cite the sources, using MLA 8 protocol.
* In what way(s) do the sources differ in their coverage? Again, be specific, with quotes.
* Consider whether the understanding you have is different from the understanding you described when this exercise first started. If it is different, how and why? If it is not changed, why not?

Here are recommended sources for your examination:

On Air and Online:	Print and Online:	Aggregators:
BBC	Heritage Foundation	Reuters
Bloomberg	American Enterprise Institute	Associated Press
CNN Student	*Washington Post*	Allsides
NPR	*New York Times*	Google News
Al Jazeera	*Boston Globe*	
	Chicago Tribune	
	The Atlantic	
	The Guardian (UK)	
	Wall Street Journal	
	LA Times	

Please select specific media outlets to examine—do not grab stories off aggregators like Google News or Yahoo without verifying the source from which it is being drawn.

Phase II

Joining the media conversation:

Option 1

On Friday evenings, during the "Week in Politics" segment of their *All Things Considered* broadcast, NPR invites news commentators from different ends of the political spectrum, such as E. J. Dionne of *The Washington Post* and David Brooks of the *New York Times*, to discuss the week's news ("Week in Politics"). Dionne is slightly left of center, and Brooks is slightly right. David Brooks also appears on the PBS *NewsHour*, where he discusses the week's wrap-up of news with Mark Shields.

Listen to one or more of these broadcasts and write the script for a point–counter point broadcast about the issue you have tracked for the last few weeks.

Option 2

On the Media is an NPR program that reviews how different media outlets have reported different stories and analyzes how the method of reporting can or could affect the impact or meaning of the event or story (*On the Media*). Listen to this broadcast on the radio or online, and write an analysis of your issue through the lens of how the media coverage impacts the listeners understanding and viewpoint.

Option 3

Each week watch *The Week in Rap*; at the end of your media watch journaling and after you have written your final reflection, you can create the rap that explores and explains the issue and the different interpretations of why and how it is important. Video- or audio-record your rap; play it for the class.

REFERENCES

On the Media. WNYC Studios. Accessed January 10, 2018. https://www.wnyc.org /shows/otm.

"Week in Politics." National Public Radio. Accessed January 10, 2010. http://npr .org/2017/05/19/529175716/week-in-politics-fallout-continues-over-firing -of-fbi-director-comey/.

"Week in Rap." *Flocabulary*. Accessed January 10, 2018. https://www.flocabulary .com/topics/week-in-rap.

Overcoming Student Resistance to Close Reading

An assured experience or common assessment (depending on your preferred lingo) for New Canaan High School ninth-grade students is a lengthy research project based on Jared Diamond's *Collapse.* Inspired by this mentor text, students research, create infographics, present to their peers, and write about the health and future prospects of our civilization. The problem our colleague was lamenting was that students were, at best, skimming the mentor text. At worst, they were randomly choosing excerpts to share before jumping ahead to the creation portions of the project. Needless to say, without a close reading of Diamond, the final presentations will be superficial and generic. So our colleague's question was twofold: (1) Why aren't they reading? (2) How can I get them to read?

Here are some recommendations for encouraging students to invest meaningfully in a close reading.

Strategy 1: Chunk It!

For this project in particular, we suggested a restructuring of the student groupings and tasks. As the project is designed now, students work in pairs with each pair presenting their reading about one of 12 different societies. Instead, we suggested, focus only on six civilizations and have four students assigned to a society with two of them responsible for presenting the reading about that society to the class and the other two responsible for critiquing the presentation based on their reading of the same text. They can do this in a fishbowl, so the rest of the class is learning the content and how to be critical friends.

We surmised that one reason students weren't reading was because they were given, all at once, the entire scope of the exercise from the initial reading assignment to the final stage that was still weeks away. Students were jumping to the product and skipping the process because they needed more scaffolding. Thus, we suggested putting them into groups and giving them the reading assignment as a discrete exercise. Keep their focus in the moment.

Strategy 2: Dialectical Notebook

Even if the assignment was scaffolded, Diamond's texts have a Lexile Measure of about 1400. Students need specific support to unpack the text. To remedy such an issue, here are other suggestions:

Students could keep a dialectical (double-entry) notebook while reading. There are lots of models of these notebooks. Some are basic and have one column designated for student summary of an aspect of the text and the other for student questions based on those summaries. Others give different column headings like "Point of View" or "Comparison," which prompt students to think critically and analytically about what they are reading.

Strategy 3: Lit Circles

In nonfiction lit circles, students are assigned a focus while reading. They then meet in small groups to share the conclusions they reach, given their individual focus, and discuss the importance of the reading evidence and insights. Reading roles can be adapted to different texts and types of media. Here are some suggested ones:

- Questioner: What would you ask the people in the passage if you could? Why?
- Connector: Of what are you reminded when you read this passage (a book, movie, TV show, current event, etc.)? Why?
- Wonderer: What do you want to know about this situation? Why?
- Predictor: What do you think the outcome of the conflict will be? Explain.
- Passage picker: Select the passage you think is key to understanding the text. Explain its importance.

Strategy 4: Partner Read

Partner annotations is a favorite tool when a text can be shared digitally. For example, in a Google Doc, two students can share a text and annotate it by inserting comments. When a student highlights a portion of the text she/he thinks is important, she/he can add a comment about why it is important, questions it raises, connections to other issues, and so on. Paired students can respond to each other's annotations, thereby carrying on a dialogue about the text in the margins.

Some of these strategies can be combined to further enhance student close reading. Consider asking students to keep a dialectical notebook using the reading roles as column headings and then bring that notebook to share in a lit circle discussion!

Happy reading!

7

Citations Are a Tool for Source Evaluation

It may seem as though a bibliography is a fairly superficial instrument to measure student learning, but it can reveal a great deal about students' approach to the research process.

For example, when researching how today's nations have been impacted by a legacy of imperialism, currency is of paramount concern. When we see bibliographies featuring books such as *Iraq: a Country Study* or *Libya since Independence* with publication dates of 1998 or earlier, it raises questions. Those books do not exist in our library's collection. We would have removed them years ago as it would be hypocritical for us to carry such outdated materials while instructing students to focus on resource currency. A quick search for those resources reveals that they refer to book reviews published in academic journals that are indexed in our databases.

What does teaching students how to create correct citations and bibliographies have to do with news literacy? Two things: not much and quite a bit. On the surface, creating a list of consulted resources seems like a mechanical, lower-order thinking task, but creating citations involves resource evaluation. The following chart cross-walks Essential Questions (EQs) with the nine Modern Language Association (MLA) elements of a citation, and the CRAAP Test. The citation seldom helps learners evaluate the accuracy of their source, but it does tell them something about currency, relevance, authority, and purpose. Creating a citation will not help researchers evaluate a resource as a stand-alone activity, but it will help learners think more analytically about what they are consulting.

Essential Question (EQ) about the Resource	MLA 8 Element	CRAAP Test Alignment
Who wrote it?	#1–Author	Authority
What is it?	#2—Title of Source	Relevance
Where is it warehoused?	#3—Container	Purpose
Who else was involved in it?	#4—Additional contributors	Authority
Where in its sequence of iterations does this one fall?	#5—Version	Currency
Does it represent one part of an ongoing series?	#6—Number	Currency
Who put it out there?	#7—Publisher	Purpose
When was it created and/or published?	#8—Date of Publication	Currency
How can I find it again?	#9—Location	

Students should also use their bibliographies to reflect on their research process holistically. Reviewing a bibliography prompts questions such as:

- Does this bibliography demonstrate that I progressed through the research process?
- Did my research question lead me to the resources I used? If not, where is the disconnect?
- What is the relationship between my resources? Do they complement one another, or are they redundant?
- What types of resources have I included (e.g., news, scholarly research, statistical information, deep-dive texts such as books, primary sources, etc.)?
- Does my list include facts, anecdotes, and opinions?
- Does this research feature a spectrum of points of view?
- Do my resources align with my thesis statement?
- Are there gaps in my research? What are they?

Learning, practicing, and perfecting research documentation habituates students to reviewing author bios, reading "About Us" pages, checking dates, and deconstructing URLs. This goes a long way toward sharpening students' skepticism—a disposition that serves researchers brilliantly.

Through an exit ticket for an English research assignment at New Canaan High School, students who had relied exclusively upon online citation generators in middle school expressed frustration at how little they knew about creating bibliographies once their teacher required them to create error-free bibliographies from scratch.

These frustrations reveal what students fail to learn from online citation generators that claim to create accurate bibliographies from copy-and-pasted URLs. Based on this feedback, New Canaan High School shifted away from such online tools and implemented a flipped learning program designed to show students how to create MLA 8 bibliographies. The system is adaptable and replicable across grades 4 through 12 and could also be used in higher education. While some parts are available on the open Web, the assessments are exclusively shared here.

To better explain what was developed for New Canaan High School students and what is shared in the pages that follow, it might be helpful to explain how it was developed. We will briefly share what we learned on our journey.

Creating an MLA Help Guide seemed like a logical first step. It was clear that some students wanted to learn how to cite sources but were not sure how to learn that. When MLA 8 was first released in April 2016, there was a catch-up period during which trustworthy and accurate portals such as NoodleTools and Purdue University's Online Writing Lab (OWL) were adding updated content. Understandably, they were not as comprehensive as their earlier iterations, which had taken seven years to populate. New Canaan High School created one that could fill the vacuum for its learning community. Packed with instructional resources such as the MLA 8 Infographic, grew quickly—too quickly for students to efficiently find what they needed. (See Figure 7.1.)

There was a lot of scrolling involved, and it became apparent that only the most motivated students were using it as a reference. We knew that we needed to migrate to a nesting-centric portal such as LibGuides (http://bit.ly/keys2 newslit7A), but until then we needed to incentivize students to use what we had.

Thus the Library Bibliography Feedback Service (LBFS) was implemented. Students were invited to submit bibliographies for review on specific days of the week, and librarians would provide speedy feedback (usually within 24 hours) to students before they handed their research assignment in to the classroom teacher. After librarians pitched this new library service at a faculty meeting, teachers eagerly instructed their students to use it. A comprehensive comment bank (Appendix 7A) helped streamline the review process. Students would include a shared link to their Google Docs bibliography through a Google Form entry, then librarians would open the link from the response spreadsheet and ascribe comments from the list, which was embedded as a drop-down menu within cells of the spreadsheet.

Over the course of two months, librarians using this system reviewed 380 bibliographies. This experience provided a goldmine of data. Some of it was building specific (e.g., individual student growth), but much of the data could be used to predict how students in other learning communities might perform on a similar assignment. We learned that there were common mistakes. (See Figure 7.2.)

For example, 33 percent of students formatted their page incorrectly. Jessica Browner, a New Canaan High School Social Studies teacher, devised the following acronym to help her students remember the basic formatting rules: Bibliographies are HARD (header, alphabetized, reverse indent, double-spaced).

The data established a correlation between librarian instruction and student performance. We compared two classes tackling the same inquiry challenge in the same course (different teacher) but with differences in time devoted to library instruction. On average, a regular section English class that received 47 minutes of librarian instruction outperformed by 23 percent an honors English class that did not receive librarian instruction. The librarian instruction for that task included a walk-through of the MLA 8 Help Page.

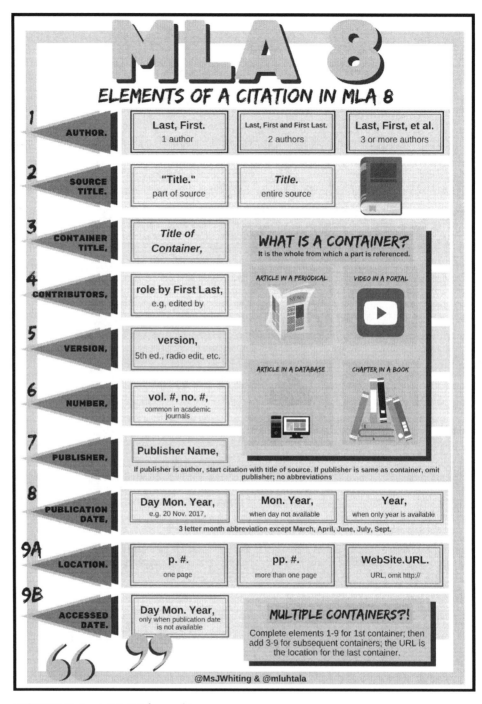

FIGURE 7.1 MLA 8 Infographic.

Percent	Comment
33%	#1 Page format—Format: Center the header.
32%	#8 Citations—Punctuation: Problems with punctuation or spacing
23%	#4 Citations—Capitalization: Title case in article, book titles, and authors
23%	#10 Citations—Extra information: There is extra information.
22%	#6 Citations—Date of access: Use date of access when you cannot find the publication date.
22%	#9 Citations—Missing information: Cannot tell what kind of resource this is from the citation (e.g., magazine, journal, newspaper, website)
22%	#5 Citations—Sequence: Items are in the wrong sequence.
22%	#3 Citations—Abbreviations: Avoid abbreviations and acronyms for organization names. Spell things out.
21%	#16 Container (element 3)—Italicizing: Italicize the names of containers (databases and periodical names).
18%	#23 Date of publication (element 8)—Date format: Day Month Year. Abbreviate months to 3 letters, followed by a period except May, June, July, and September, which is abbreviated to 4 letters (Sept.).
18%	#24 Location (element 9)—URL: Delete http:// and omit < >.
17%	#13 Author (element 1)—Corporate authors: Do not reverse corporate authors (e.g., Associated Press is correct; not Press, Associated).
14%	#29 Publisher (element 7)—Periodicals: Omit publisher information when citing periodicals.
15%	#24 Location (element 9)—URL: Missing URLs
12%	#2 Page format—Citation arrangement: Do not number, categorize, or bullet your source list.
12%	#24 Location (element 9)—URL: Remove hyperlinks so that the document is consistently in black ink and there is no underlining.
11%	#16 Container (element 3)—Periodicals: Include publication name, volume (when available), issue (when available), date of publication, and page number(s).
10%	#22 Publisher (element 7)—Websites: Include correct publisher for websites and books (including e-books).
10%	#14 Author (element 1)—Sequence: Last name first, first name last
10%	#15 Title of Source (element 2)—Italicizing vs. quotes: Part of a larger source in quotations, entire source in italics

FIGURE 7.2   Common Bibliography Mistakes.

It became clear that bibliographies requiring more than four comments from the comment bank required far more "grading" time. Library Bibliography Feedback Service (LBFS), which was valuable to the entire learning community as evidenced by the number and range of submissions, was sustainable only if the quality of student work improved significantly. Using much of the content from the MLA 8 Help Page, we created 14 mini slides shows, which we turned into video tutorials. There is one mini tutorial for each of the nine MLA 8 elements, preceded by an introduction, and these were followed by four additional tutorials (date of access, abbreviations, and two on page formatting). Scaffolding the instruction into 1- to 2-minute videos allowed students to easily access and revisit a concept they need to review. The videos are accessible through the library's YouTube channel (http://bit.ly/keys2newslit7C), but after piloting the rollout in Nearpod, an interactive presentation and assessment tool, we decided that Moodle, an open-source learning management system, would produce the best data for us to analyze, given that we planned to administer the instrument to all students in grades 9–11 (at New Canaan High School, 12th-grade students cite sources following APA guidelines). Thus we embedded the slides and videos in Moodle. While that content is accessible to the public via the guest user button, the assessments are not. Each learning module ends with a Check for Understanding or a mini quiz (Appendix 7B). Most of these are comprised of a single question. We chose to separate them to give students an opportunity to reattempt each question without having to retake the entire assessment. Just as importantly, we wanted to incorporate digital badges into the instructional program, and badges can be awarded only for the completion of a task, not parts of a larger task.

Once learners complete the 14 student-paced learning modules, the teacher or librarian administers a 12-question quiz (Appendix 7C). Students can attempt this quiz only once (unless their attempt is cleared and reset by a teacher). Students passing the quiz with a score of 75 or higher (out of 100) earn their 15th badge. Once they have all 15 badges, they can submit bibliographies for librarian feedback. The librarian checks students' badge status before reviewing their work. This makes it possible to provide a valuable service to students while keeping the grading task manageable for librarian(s). A checkbric facilitates bibliography scoring (Appendix 7D).

Based on a small sampling of 9th-grade bibliography scores, data indicates that the student-paced instructional models, incentivized by digital badges, have a positive impact on student work. As Figure 7.3 indicates, 60 percent of 9th graders who scored higher than 95 percent on the final quiz earned a 75 percent or higher grade on their first bibliography submission, whereas only 22 percent of those who scored below a 75 percent on the quiz scored 75 percent or higher on their bibliography.

MLA 8 Quiz Score	Percent of Students Who Met Goal on Bibliography
95–100	60%
85–94	54%
75–84	41%
below 75	22%

Note: This is for a 9th-grade class, and these were the first comprehensive bibliographies.

FIGURE 7.3 Quiz and Bibliography Scores.

APPENDIX 7A: BIBLIOGRAPHY FEEDBACK COMMENT BANK

1. Page format—**Format**:
   a. Bibliography/Works Cited list is on its own page following the complete research task (essay, presentation, graphic, etc.)
   b. Size 12 font
   c. Times New Roman font
   d. Double-spaced
   e. No lines skipped between citations
   f. Left margin aligned
   g. Hanging indents
   h. Alphabetized according to first word in citations (after "a," "an," and "the")

   For more details, visit <http://bit.ly/MLA8comment1and2>.
   Review the full comment bank at <http://bit.ly/MLA8comments>.

2. Page format—**List**: Alphabetize list according to the first word in your citations after "A," "An," or "The,"; align left; do not number or categorize or bullet your sources.

   For more details, visit <http://bit.ly/MLA8comment1and2>.
   Review the full comment bank at <http://bit.ly/MLA8comments>.

3. Citations—**Abbreviations**: No abbreviations. Spell it out (e.g., TED is Technology, Engineering, and Design [not TED Talk!], NPR is National Public Radio; BBC is British Broadcasting Corporation; CNN is Cable News Network).

   For more details, visit <https://bit.ly/MLA8comment3>.
   Review the full comment bank at <http://bit.ly/MLA8comments>.

4. Citations—**Capitalization**: Use title case for authors, article titles, containers, and publishers.

   For more details, visit <http://bit.ly/MLA8comment4>.
   Review the full comment bank at <http://bit.ly/MLA8comments>.

5. Citations—**Sequence**: Some elements are in the wrong sequence.

   For more details, visit <http://bit.ly/MLA8comment5and10>.
   Review the full comment bank at <http://bit.ly/MLA8comments>.

6. Citations—**Date of Access**: Use date of access only when you cannot find the publication date for an Internet source. Date of access follows URL and a period.

   For more details, visit <http://bit.ly/MLA8comment6>.
   Review the full comment bank at <http://bit.ly/MLA8comments>.

7. Citations—**Citation style**: Change into MLA 8. You may have used MLA 7 (usually happens in EasyBib. Indicators include Web., Print., n.p., n.d.) or APA (usually happens when the wrong database citation is copied and pasted. Indicators include a date in parentheses, the omission of **vol. and no.** before the volume and issue numbers).

   For more details, visit <http://bit.ly/MLA8comment7>.
   Review the full comment bank at <http://bit.ly/MLA8comments>.

8. Citations—**Punctuation**: Problems with punctuation or spacing between the elements. This may mean that a period(s) at the end of the citation or before starting the second container was (were) left out.

   Review the full comment bank at <http://bit.ly/MLA8comment8>.
   Review the full comment bank at <http://bit.ly/MLA8comments>.

9. Citations—**Missing information**: A properly cited source implicitly identifies the resource type (e.g., magazine, journal, newspaper, website, book, e-book, etc.). This one does not.

   Review the full comment bank at <http://bit.ly/MLA8comment9>.
   Review the full comment bank at <http://bit.ly/MLA8comments>.

10. Citations—**Extra information**: Citations include more information than what is called for in MLA 8. Check required nine elements. Often, when students copy and paste the URL into EasyBib to create a citation, the generator lumps extra information into the title.

    For more details, visit <http://bit.ly/MLA8comment5and10>.
    Review the full comment bank at <http://bit.ly/MLA8comments>.

11. Citations—**Symbols**: Avoid using math symbols (+ or |) in citations. This usually happens when EasyBib fails to separate elements 2 (Title of Source) and 3 (Container). They get lumped together in quotation marks with the | as a divider. Then the software generates a redundant citation because the website name is repeated.

    For more details, visit <http://bit.ly/MLA8comment11>.
    Review the full comment bank at <http://bit.ly/MLA8comments>.

12. Citations—**DOI**: Omit DOI. The publisher assigns a Digital Object Identifier (DOI) when your article is published and made available electronically. It is used as a substitute for the URL. You may use this in college, but it is to be replaced by a URL at NCHS.

    For more details, visit <http://bit.ly/MLA8comment12>.
    Review the full comment bank at <http://bit.ly/MLA8comments>.

13. Author (element 1)—**Corporate author**: Do not reverse corporate author names. Associated Press is correct (not Press, Associated). A corporate author is a tricky concept. The Central Intelligence Agency is the author of *The World Factbook*, but a periodical such as the *New York Times* is never listed as a corporate author. On the other hand, the Associated Press, which is a news agency, is a corporate author. United States government agencies are tricky. Use the agency as a corporate author and the United States as the publisher. There are often agencies within agencies (e.g., Choose My Plate → Center for Nutrition Policy and Promotion → Department of Agriculture → United States). This complicates the container listing. If you are confused, ask for help.

   Also, several websites provide incorrect recommendations for citations. Biography.com, History.com, and Encyclopaedia Britannica are just three of the many websites that lead students astray on citations. This is especially relevant when it comes to the corporate author piece. History.com suggests that you include "History.com Staff" as the corporate author. Encyclopedia Britannica makes a similar recommendation on their Cite link. Don't do what they tell you!

   For more details, visit <http://bit.ly/MLA8comment13>.
   Review the full comment bank at <http://bit.ly/MLA8comments>.

14. Author (element 1)—**Sequence**: Last name first, first name last for one author. For two authors, last name first, first name last, then first name first, last name last. For three or more authors, include only first author followed by et al. Place name suffixes after middle name or first name if there is no middle name.

   For more details, visit <http://bit.ly/MLA8comment14>.
   Review the full comment bank at <http://bit.ly/MLA8comments>.

15. Title of Source (element 2)—**Italicizing vs. quotes**: If the title is part of a larger source, write it in quotation marks. If the entire source is being used, the title is written in italics.

   For more details, visit <http://bit.ly/MLA8comment15>.
   Review the full comment bank at <http://bit.ly/MLA8comments>.

16. Container (element 3)—A web page is the "title"; a website is a container. **Italicize** the names of containers (e.g., books, periodicals, and databases).

   For more details, visit <http://bit.ly/MLA8comment16>.
   Review the full comment bank at <http://bit.ly/MLA8comments>.

17. Container (element 3)—There can be **multiple containers**. Database names are often included as second or third containers. When there

are multiple containers, add elements 1–9 first, followed by a period; then add elements 3–9 as many times as you need.

For more details, visit <http://bit.ly/MLA8comment17>.
Review the full comment bank at <http://bit.ly/MLA8comments>.

18. Additional contributor (element 4)—Describe the contributor's **role** where appropriate (e.g., edited by, directed by, translated by, performed by, etc.). Capitalize the first letter in the role if it follows a period, but start with a lowercase letter if it follows a comma. The contributor name is written first name first and last name last. Use the et al. abbreviation when there are more than two contributors.

For more details, visit <http://bit.ly/MLA8comment18>.
Review the full comment bank at <http://bit.ly/MLA8comments>.

19. Version (element 5)—Version: This element helps to identify **e-books**. Other **versions** could include an edition, director's cut, late edition, radio edit, and so on.

For more details, visit <http://bit.ly/MLA8comment19>.
Review the full comment bank at <http://bit.ly/MLA8comments>.

20. Number (element 6)—Include number information when resource is released **periodically** (e.g., an academic journal, episode in a program, etc.) or **part** of a multivolume work (e.g., an encyclopedia or other reference work). Abbreviate vol._, no._, (insert correct number in blank spaces!).

For more details, visit <http://bit.ly/MLA8comment20>.
Review the full comment bank at <http://bit.ly/MLA8comments>.

21. Publisher (element 7)—**When to include**: Do *not* include publisher information when citing newspapers, magazines, and journals. *Do* thoroughly investigate the publisher on all websites (e.g., "About Us" page, breadcrumbs, root URL [what ends with the .com/.edu/.gov /.org, etc.], "Contact," "Mission," etc.), but check the rules about redundancy before including it in the citation. Publisher *must* be included in book citations (print *and* e-books). (Link is on website.)

For more details, visit <http://bit.ly/MLA8comment21>.
Review the full comment bank at <http://bit.ly/MLA8comments>.

22. Publisher (element 7)—**Redundancy**: If author and publisher are the same, omit the author. If the webpage name and the website name are the same (which is very unusual, so look twice!), include only the website as title in italics. If the website and its publisher share the same name (which is common), omit the publisher and include the container

only. Do not repeat information in the citation. Click here for more information:

For more details, visit <http://bit.ly/MLA8comment22>.
Review the full comment bank at <http://bit.ly/MLA8comments>.

23. Date of publication (element 8)—**Date format**: Dates are Day Mon. Year. Abbreviate all months to three letters followed by a period except May, June, and July, which are written in their entirety, and September, which is (oddly) abbreviated as "Sept."

For more details, visit <http://bit.ly/MLA8comment23>.
Review the full comment bank at <http://bit.ly/MLA8comments>.

24. Location (element 9)—**URLs**: Remove hyperlinks, delete http://, and omit "greater than" and "less than" symbols <>. Use permalinks wherever possible (e.g., New York Times and EBSCO).

For more details, visit <http://bit.ly/MLA8comment24>.
Review the full comment bank at <http://bit.ly/MLA8comments>.

25. Location (element 9)—**Pages**: Include page number or range. Abbreviate the word page (singular) as p. and pages (plural) as pp. Use lowercase letters for abbreviations.

For more details, visit <http://bit.ly/MLA8comment25>.
Review the full comment bank at <http://bit.ly/MLA8comments>.

26. Research—**Reference**: You have too many encyclopedic resources in this bibliography.

For more details, visit <http://bit.ly/MLA8comment26>.
Review the full comment bank at <http://bit.ly/MLA8comments>.

27. Research—**Alignment**: At least one source does not meet one or more of the required research expectations for this assignment.

For more details, visit <http://bit.ly/MLA8comment27>.
Review the full comment bank at <http://bit.ly/MLA8comments>.

28. Research—**Range**: The resource collection lacks range. Consider including expert opinion, academic journals, primary sources, research studies, statistical analysis, and/or public opinion surveys. What you have here would not meet passing criteria in college. Academics want to see the work of academics in works cited lists. A list of mainstream news publications will suggest that you did not dig deeply enough into your topic.

For more details, visit <http://bit.ly/MLA8comment28>.
Review the full comment bank at <http://bit.ly/MLA8comments>.

29. **Periodicals** (newspapers, magazines, journals): It is essential that you include as many of the following as are available
    a. Publication name (must be included!)
    b. Volume
    c. Issue
    d. Date of publication (must be included!)
    e. Location (URL or page—or both!)

    For more details, visit <http://bit.ly/MLA8comment29>.
    Review the full comment bank at <http://bit.ly/MLA8comments>.

30. **Domain name extension**: Omit domain extensions from website names (.org, .com, .edu, etc.).

    For more details, visit <http://bit.ly/MLA8comment30>.
    Review the full comment bank at <http://bit.ly/MLA8comments>.

APPENDIX 7B: MLA 8 SELF-GUIDED INSTRUCTION—CHECKS

INTRODUCTION

1. _____ **MLA 8 breaks down all citations, from print books to Tweets, into nine elements.**
   A. True
   B. False

AUTHOR

2. _____ **Which of the following citations lists the "Author" information INCORRECTLY (MLA 8 element #1 - Author)? [Click on image to the left of this text to see the detailed choices.]**
   A. Associated Press. "Yates Calls Flynn's Manner 'Problematic'." *Times Video,* New York Times, 8 May 2017, nyti.ms/2pYiUw2.
   B. Coerver, Don M., et al. *Mexico an Encyclopedia of Contemporary Culture and History.* e-Book, ABC-CLIO, 2004.
   C. Coerver, Don M., Suzanne B. Pasztor, and Robert Buffington. *Mexico an Encyclopedia of Contemporary Culture and History.* e-Book, ABC-CLIO, 2004.
   D. U.S. Department of Health & Human Services. "World Map of Areas with Risk of Zika." *Center for Disease Control,* United States, 6 Sept. 2017, wwwnc.cdc.gov/travel/page/world-map-areas-with-zika.

TITLE

3. _____ **Which of the following citations lists the "Title" information CORRECTLY (MLA 8 element #2 - Title)? [Click on image to the left of this text to see the detailed choices.]**
   A. Diamond, Jared. *Norse Greenland's End.* "Collapse: How Societies Choose to Fail or Succeed." Viking, 2005, pp. 211–247.
   B. Diamond, Jared. "*Norse Greenland's End.*" Collapse: How Societies Choose to Fail or Succeed, Viking, 2005, pp. 211–247.
   C. Diamond, Jared. Norse Greenland's End. Collapse: How Societies Choose to Fail or Succeed, "*Viking,*" 2005, pp. 211–247.
   D. Diamond, Jared. "Norse Greenland's End." *Collapse: How Societies Choose to Fail or Succeed,* Viking, 2005, pp. 211–247.

CONTAINER

4. _____ **A citation can have 3 or more containers.**
   A. True
   B. False

5. _____ **When there are several containers, cite elements 1-9, and end with a period before adding additional elements 3-9.**
   A. True
   B. False

6. _____ **A container is the same thing as a publisher.**
   A. True
   B. False

7. _____ **Which one of the following citations identifies in bold red font the "Container(s)" INCORRECTLY (MLA 8 element #3 - Container)? [Click on image to the left of this text to see the detailed choices.]**
   A. "India's Chronic Battle with Malnutrition." Blog. *New York Times*, 12 Jan. 2012, india.blogs.nytimes.com/2012/01/12/indias-chronic -battle-with-malnutrition/.
   B. "McCain Slams Putin in Fiery Senate Speech." *Cable News Network*, Turner Broadcasting System, 7 Feb. 2017. *YouTube*, youtube/bJhRFTnwSvc.
   C. Nagel, James. "Kate Chopin's Bayou Folk." *Race and Culture in New Orleans Stories: Kate Chopin, Grace King, Alice Dunbar-Nelson, and George Washington Cable*. University Alabama Press, 2014, pp. 119–159. *EBSCOhost*, search.ebscohost.com/login.aspx ?direct=true&AuthType=shib&db=e000xna&AN=681638&site=eds -live&custid=s9378636.
   D. Roop, Peter, and Connie. "Mike King, Jr. Gets a New Name." *Let's Dream, Martin Luther King, Jr.!* **Scholastic**, 2004.

8. _____ **Highlight what SHOULD be italicized as the "Container(s)" in the following citations (MLA 8 element #3 - Container). [Click on image to the left of this text to see the detailed choices.]**
   A. "Helicopter Parents: You're Grounded!" New York Times, 22 Oct. 2014, p. A26. EBSCOhost, search.ebscohost.com/login.aspx?direct =true&AuthType=shib&db=edsgwh&AN=edsgcl.386822360&site =eds-live&custid=s9378636.
   B. "McCain Slams Putin in Fiery Senate Speech." Cable News Network, Turner Broadcasting System, 7 Feb. 2017. YouTube, you tube/bJhRFTnwSvc.
   C. Noonan, Peggy. "Democracy Is Not Your Plaything." Wall Street Journal, 18 May 2017, www.wsj.com/articles/democracy-is-not -your-plaything-1495149082?tesla=y.
   D. Rodgers, Lucy, et al. "Syria: The Story of the Conflict." BBC News: The Middle East, British Broadcasting Corporation, 11 March, 2016, www.bbc.com/news/world-middle-east-26116868.

OTHER CONTRIBUTORS

9. _____ Which of the following citations includes "Other Contributor" information (MLA 8 element #4 - Other Contributor)? [Click on image to the left of this text to see the detailed choices.]
   A. Danzer, Gerald, et al. "The Living Constitution." *The Americans*, McDougal Littell, 2007, pp.152–179.
   B. Editorial Board. "How to Tell Truth from Fiction in the Age of Fake News." *Chicago Tribune*, 21 Nov. 2016, www.chicagotribune.com /news/opinion/editorials/ct-fake-news-facebook-edit-1120-md -20161118-story.html.
   C. Houston, Lynn M. "Diet and Nutrition." *Food Culture in the Caribbean*, edited by Ken Albala. Greenwood Press, 2005, pp. 141–146.
   D. Menzel, Peter, and Faith D'Alusio. "China: Xu Zhipeng the Extreme Gamer." *What I Eat: Around the World in 80 Diets*. Ten Speed Press, 2005, pp. 47–49.

VERSION

10. _____ Which of the following TWO citations includes "Version" information (MLA 8 element #5 - Version)? [Click on image to the left of this text to see the detailed choices.]
   A. Ellis, Elisabeth Gaynor and Anthony Esler, "The Soviet Union: Rise and Fall of a Superpower." *World History: Connections to Today*, Prentice Hall, 2005, pp. 843–847, 887.
   B. Hewitt, Paul. "Energy." *Conceptual Physics*, 12th ed., Addison-Wesley, 2014, pp. 103–121.
   C. Kemp, Donna R. "Deinstitutionalization." *Mental Health in America: A Reference Handbook*, e-Book, ABC-CLIO, 2007.
   D. Marston, Daniel. "Army, Partition, and the Punjab Boundary Force, 1945–1947." *War in History*, vol. 16, no. 4, Nov. 2009, pp. 469–505. *Explora*, search.ebscohost.com/login.aspx?direct=true&AuthType =shib&db=aph&AN=44287983&custid=s9378636.

NUMBER

11. _____ Which of the following citations includes "Number" information (MLA 8 element #6 - Number)? [Click on image to the left of this text to see the detailed choices.]
   A. Ellis, Elisabeth Gaynor, and Anthony Esler, "The Soviet Union: Rise and Fall of a Superpower." *World History: Connections to Today*, Prentice Hall, 2005, pp. 843–847, 887.
   B. Hewitt, Paul. "Energy." *Conceptual Physics*, 12th ed., Addison-Wesley, 2014, pp. 103–121.
   C. Kemp, Donna R. "Deinstitutionalization." *Mental Health in America: A Reference Handbook*, e-Book, ABC-CLIO, 2007.

D. Marston, Daniel. "Army, Partition, and the Punjab Boundary Force, 1945–1947." *War in History*, vol. 16, no. 4, Nov. 2009, pp. 469–505. *Explora*, search.ebscohost.com/login.aspx?direct=true&AuthType =shib&db=aph&AN=44287983&custid=s9378636.

PUBLISHER

12. _____Which of the following **citations lists the "Publisher" information INCORRECTLY (MLA 8 element #7 - Publisher)? [Click on image to the left of this text to see the detailed choices.]**
    A. Carr, Nicholas. "Is Google Making Us Stupid?" *Atlantic*, July/ Aug. 2008, www.theatlantic.com/magazine/archive/2008/07/is -google-making-us-stupid/306868.
    B. Friedman, Thomas. "The New Untouchables." *New York Times*, The New York Times Company. 21 Oct. 2009, nyti.ms/2mxj9gx. Editorial.
    C. Trabant, Gigi. "Working for Time Life in the 1960s." interviewed by Michelle Luhtala, *StoryCorps*, 23 Feb. 2017.
    D. "Why Are Colleges Really Going Test-Optional?" *Morning Edition*, National Public Radio, 3 Sept. 2015. *Opposing Viewpoints in Context*, link.galegroup.com/apps/doc/A429371737/OVIC?u=new11 256&xid=5afeb738.

DATE

13. _____ **Which citation displays the format for the "Date of Publication" information CORRECTLY (MLA 8 element #8 - Date of Publication)?**
    A. 10 Feb. 2017
    B. Feb. 10 2017
    C. 10 Feb, 2017
    D. Feb 10, 2017

14. _____ **Which of the following citations lists the "Date of Publication" information INCORRECTLY (MLA 8 element #8—Date of Publication)? [Click on image to the left of this text to see the detailed choices.]**
    A. @WEganprincipal. "Thank you @NCHS_CT community for a wonderful Open House this evening. It was great to see so many parents out this evening." *Twitter*, 25 Sept. 2017 9:30 p.m., twitter.com /WEganprincipal/status/912508668461092865.
    B. Sifferlin, Alexandra. "When A Guy Gets An Eating Disorder." *Time*, 8 April 2014, time.com/54158/when-a-guy-gets-an-eating -disorder.
    C. Wiedeman, Reeves. "The Sandy Hook Hoax." *New York*, 5 Sept. 2016, nymag.com/daily/intelligencer/2016/09/the-sandy-hook-hoax .html.

D. Blow, Charles M. "Blood in the Water." *New York Times*, May 22, 2017, p. A25. *National Newspapers Core*, search.proquest.com/doc view/1900777558?accountid=4973.

LOCATION

15. _____ **Location refers to a URL for Internet sources and a page number or page range for print resources.**
   A. True
   B. False

16. _____ **Which TWO of the following citations cite the "Location" information CORRECTLY (MLA 8 element #9 - Location)? [Click on image to the left of this text to see the detailed choices.]**
   A. "The False Identity Card of Vladka Meed." *United States Holocaust Museum*, New York Times, 24 Nov. 2012, nyti.ms/2mFg0e6.
   B. "League of German Girls in the Hitler Youth (c. 1936)." *Spartacus Educational*, 2016, spartacus-educational.com/2WWgirls.htm.
   C. Rodgers, Lucy, et al. "Syria: The Story of the Conflict." *BBC News: The Middle East*, British Broadcasting Corporation, 11 March, 2016, http://www.bbc.com/news/world-middle-east-26116868.
   D. Zimmer, Carl. "The Purpose of Sleep? to Forget, Scientists Say." *New York Times*, late edition, 7 Feb. 2017, Science sec., p. 5.

DATE OF ACCESS

17. _____ **The date of access MUST be included when**
   A. There is no location
   B. There is no date of location
   C. There is no date of publication
   D. There is no publisher location

ABBREVIATIONS

18. _____ **Complete the names of popular media sites in the numbered list below by writing the letter labeling the correct word in the space where it belongs.**

A. Engineering	**B.** Public	**C.** Microsoft
D. Service	**E.** British	**F.** Corporation
G. Technology	**H.** Network	**I.** Design
J. National	**K.** Radio	**L.** Broadcasting

NPR: **1.** _____ Public _____
BBC: **2.** _____ Broadcasting _____
CNN: **3.** Cable News _____
MSNBC: **4.** _____ National _____ Company (Microsoft is out, but they kept the name. It's part of NBCNews now, which is own by Comcast)

PBS: **5.**_____ Broadcasting _____
FOX: **6.** Fox News
TED: **7.** _____ _____ and _____
Huffington Post
National Geographic

FORMATTING

19. _____ **The best way to create hanging indents is with the**
    A. Tab
    B. Space
    C. Ruler
    D. Shift

20. _____ **The "A" in the acronym H.A.R.D. refers to**
    A. Anonymous
    B. A
    C. An
    D. Alphabetized

APPENDIX 7C: BIBLIOGRAPHY QUIZ

Directions: Identify the error that best describes each footnoted mistake in this bibliography by writing the correct letter from the table in the space next to its corresponding footnote at the bottom of this page.

"Afghanistan." World History: The Modern Era,[1] *ABC-CLIO,*[2] 2017, worldhistory.abc
-clio.com/Search/Display/317188.[3]

Michael Burgan,[4] "The Soviets Arrive". *Afghanistan,* Rourke, 2009, PP.[5] 20–27. *EBSCOhost,* search.ebscohost.com/login.aspx?direct=true&AuthType=shib &db=n8h&AN=50407047&site=eds-live&custid=s9378636[6]

Dec. 27 in History: Soviet Union Begins Fruitless 10-Year Presence in Afghanistan.[7] *Abilene Reporter-News,* December 27 2013.[8] *EBSCOhost,* http://search. ebscohost.com/login.aspx?direct=true&AuthType=shib&db=edsnbk&AN=14 AF62D3E80AE290&site=eds-live&custid=s9378636.[9]

Ellis, Elisabeth Gaynor, Block, Melissa, and Anthony Esler.[10] "The Soviet Union: Rise and Fall of a Superpower." *World History: Connections to Today,* Prentice Hall, 2005, pp. 843–847, 887.

Fisher, Max, and Amanda Taub. "Why Afghanistan's War Defies Solutions." *New York Times.*[11,12]

A. Publisher: Should not be italicized	B. Location: Lowercase abbreviation for pages	C. Date: Missing date of publication
D. Author: Replace some of these names with et al.	E. Date: Day Mon. Year	F. Author: Last name first, First name last
G. Location: Omit http://	H. Title of Source: Should be in italics or quotes	I. Location: Missing Location
J. Container: Should be italicized	K. Location: Should not be hyperlinked	L. Location: End citation with a period

---

1. _____ which letter from the key best describes the footnoted mistake?
2. _____ which letter from the key best describes the footnoted mistake?
3. _____ which letter from the key best describes the footnoted mistake?
4. _____ which letter from the key best describes the footnoted mistake?
5. _____ which letter from the key best describes the footnoted mistake?
6. _____ which letter from the key best describes the footnoted mistake?
7. _____ which letter from the key best describes the footnoted mistake?
8. _____ which letter from the key best describes the footnoted mistake?
9. _____ which letter from the key best describes the footnoted mistake?
10. _____ which letter from the key best describes the footnoted mistake?
11. _____ which letter from the key best describes the footnoted mistake?
12. _____ which letter from the key best describes the footnoted mistake?

APPENDIX 7D: BIBLIOGRAPHY CHECKBRIC

Student Name:		Date:
Teacher:		Period:

Appendix 7D: BIBLIOGRAPHY CHECKBRIC

PAGE FORMAT					
Layout & List		Comment #1 bit.ly/MLA8comment1and2	Comment #2 bit.ly/MLA8comment1and2	5	0
ELEMENTS					
Element		Comment	Comment		
1 - Author		Comment #13 bit.ly/MLA8comment13	Comment #14 bit.ly/MLA8comment14	5	0
2 - Title		Comment #15 bit.ly/MLA8comment15		5	0
3 - Container		Comment #16 bit.ly/MLA8comment16	Comment #17 bit.ly/MLA8comment17	5	0
4 - Contributor		Comment #18 bit.ly/MLA8comment18		5	0
5 - Version		Comment #19 bit.ly/MLA8comment19		5	0
6 - Number		Comment #20 bit.ly/MLA8comment20		5	0
7 - Publisher		Comment #21 bit.ly/MLA8comment21	Comment #22 bit.ly/MLA8comment22	5	0
8 - Date		Comment #23 bit.ly/MLA8comment23		5	0
9 - Location		Comment #24 bit.ly/MLA8comment24	Comment #25 bit.ly/MLA8comment25	5	0
			SUBTOTAL =		
OTHER CITATION ISSUES					
Abbreviations		Comment #3 bit.ly/MLA8comment3		-1	
Capitalization		Comment #4 bit.ly/MLA8comment4		-1	
Sequence		Comment #5 bit.ly/MLA8comment5and10		-1	
Date of Access		Comment #6 bit.ly/MLA8comment6		-1	
Citation Style		Comment #7 bit.ly/MLA8comment7		-1	
Punctuation		Comment #8 bit.ly/MLA8comment8		-1	
Missing Info		Comment #9 bit.ly/MLA8comment9		-1	
Extra Info		Comment #10 bit.ly/MLA8comment5and10		-1	
Symbols		Comment #11 bit.ly/MLA8comment11		-1	
D.O.I.		Comment #12 bit.ly/MLA8comment12		-1	
Periodicals		Comment #29 bit.ly/MLA8comment29		-1	
Domain		Comment #30 bit.ly/MLA8comment30		-1	
			SUBTOTAL + 50 =		
RESEARCH ISSUES					
Reference		Comment #26 bit.ly/MLA8comment26		-12	
Alignment		Comment #27 bit.ly/MLA8comment27		-13	
Range		Comment #28 bit.ly/MLA8comment28		-12	
			TOTAL =		

Comment #1	**Comment #2**	**Comment #3**	**Comment #4**	**Comment #5**
Page layout	List	Abbreviations	Capitalization	Sequence

Comment #6	**Comment #7**	**Comment #8**	**Comment #9**	**Comment #10**
Date of acces	Citation style	Punctuation	Missing info	Extra info

Comment #11	**Comment #12**	**Comment #13**	**Comment #14**	**Comment #15**
Symbols	D.O.I.	1 - Author A	1 - Author B	2 - Title

Comment #16	**Comment #17**	**Comment #18**	**Comment #19**	**Comment #20**
3 - Container A	3 - Container B	4 - Contributor	5 - Version	6 - Number

Comment #21	**Comment #22**	**Comment #23**	**Comment #24**	**Comment #25**
7 - Publisher A	7 - Publisher B	8 - Date of Pub	9 - Location A	9 - Location B

Comment #26	**Comment #27**	**Comment #28**	**Comment #29**	**Comment #30**
Research - Reference	Research - Alignment	Research - Range	Periodicals	Domain

8

Big Takeaways

1. Fake news, alternative facts, and propaganda are not new phenomena. What is new is the capacity ordinary people have for transmitting this information and engaging in civic discourse. Social media and digital publication have empowered the citizen journalist as much as it has the misinformer and manipulator of public opinion. The skills for critically reading media in any form is essential to healthy civic activism. (See Figure 8.1.)

2. When students resist doing what you are asking—stop, resist your urge to point fingers at them and ask what is wrong with students today. Instead, reflect on what you, the teacher or librarian, are asking of the students. When teachers say to us things such as: "My students just don't learn and work the way my students did ten years ago," we say, "Right. So let's not try to teach them the same way we taught ten years ago." We consistently ask ourselves: How do our students spend their free time? When they want to know how to do something, what do they do? How do they communicate with their peers? How is that different than how they communicate with adults? Generally, currently, we answer these questions with: "They spend time with headphones in listening to music or watching videos or live chatting with friends. They watch videos that show them how to do things. They snapchat their friends and e-mail adults." Given this insight, how should we change our instruction and assessment to capitalize on what students do well and do natively? What information literacy skills do they need to exist in this environment responsibly?

3. Learning happens through reflection and revision. Absent opportunities for feedback and reconsideration of both their processes and products, students experience limited success in applying what they are supposed to be learning to real-world tasks and experiences. We don't learn something the first time we do it. We may learn a piece of it, and we certainly learn what not to do next time. There must be a next time for us to

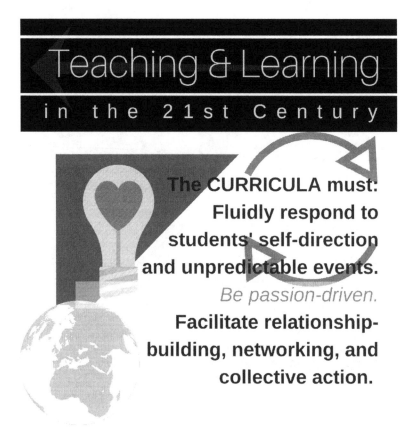

FIGURE 8.1　21st-Century Teaching and Learning Infographic.

reflect, plan, and practice new skills and approaches to solving problems. (See Figure 8.2.)

4. Learning takes time, and that is the one resource teachers complain the most about lacking. Learning is borne of struggle and struggle takes time, so we must dignify the process. Time is a resource like computers, classrooms, athletic equipment, staff members, and so on. While it may be intangible, it still should be considered in the same way other resources are considered: what are our educational priorities, and how do we allocate our resources to maximize fulfilling those priorities?

5. We are not alone in our mission to develop students' information literacy! More and more resources are being created and shared by credible agencies with educational missions and mandates. Here are a few:

SearchResearch

- Dan Russell's Blog has daily posts of creative and interesting search exercises (like scavenger hunts) you can do with your students: http://searchresearch1.blogspot.com/

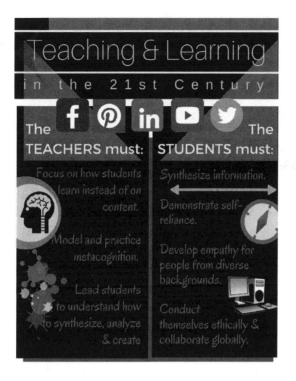

FIGURE 8.2   21st-Century Teaching and Learning Infographic.

Newseum
- http://www.newseum.org/
- http://www.newseum.org/wp-content/uploads/2014/08/education_ LCO_believeitornotLP.pdf
- ESCAPE Junk News: https://newseumed.org/activity/e-s-c-a-p-e-junk -news-mlbp/

***New York Times* Learning Network**
- https://www.nytimes.com/section/learning
- https://www.nytimes.com/2017/01/19/learning/lesson-plans/evalua ting-sources-in-a-post-truth-world-ideas-for-teaching-and-learning -about-fake-news.html
- https://static01.nyt.com/images/blogs/learning/pdf/2014/IMVAINSo urceReliabilityChecklist.pdf
- https://static01.nyt.com/images/blogs/learning/pdf/activities/Cen soringPress_NYTLN.pdf

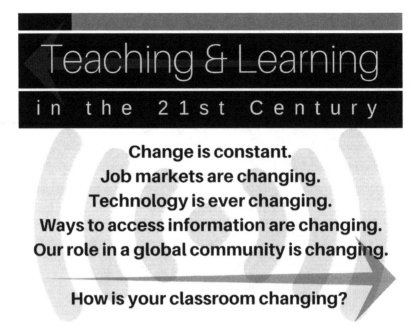

FIGURE 8.3 21st-Century Teaching and Learning Infographic.

Common Sense Media
- https://www.commonsensemedia.org/
- https://www.commonsensemedia.org/blog/how-to-spot-fake-news-and-teach-kids-to-be-media-savvy

Thinking Like Fact-Checkers
- First Draft News from Harvard University's Shorenstein Center on Media, Politics, and Public Policy:
  https://firstdraftnews.com/
- Snopes:
  https://www.snopes.com/
- Politifact:
  http://www.politifact.com/
- Hoax-Slayer:
  http://hoax-slayer.com/

Reverse Image Searching
- "13 Online Tools That Help to Verify the Authenticity of a Photo" (Stop Fake.org):
  https://www.stopfake.org/en/13-online-tools-that-help-to-verify-the-authenticity-of-a-photo/

- How to verify images and videos (First Draft News):
  https://firstdraftnews.com/are-you-a-journalist-download-this-free
  -guide-for-verifying-photos-and-videos/
- Breaking News Consumer's Handbook (WNYC):
  https://www.wnyc.org/shows/otm/handbooks
- "Educator's Guide: Types of Online Fakes" (Verification Handbook):
  http://verificationhandbook.com/additionalmaterial/types-of-online-
  fakes.php

Lesson Tools and Ideas
- "Teaching Your Students about Fake News" from Monica Brady-Myerov's
  team at Listenwise (listenwise.com):
  https://support.listenwise.com/teaching-your-students-about-fake
  -news/
- "How to Choose Your News" from Ted-Ed by Damon Brown:
  https://ed.ted.com/lessons/how-to-choose-your-news-damon-brown
- "Here's What Happens When the Readers Choose the Front Page Story"
  from NewsWhip by Paul Quigley:
  https://www.newswhip.com/2014/03/people-powered-front-pages
  -rock/
- "The Phenomenon of Fake News" from Newsela:
  https://newsela.com/text-sets/157107/fake-news
- "Media Literacy Resources" from NewseumED:
  https://newseumed.org/stack/media-literacy-resources/
- Stony Brook University Center for News Literacy Digital Resource
  Center:
  http://drc.centerfornewsliteracy.org/

6. We and our students must be digital neighbors if we are to provide them
   with purposeful guidance and instruction regarding their use and understanding of digital media. For many years, teachers have sat through faculty meetings where district lawyers have warned us about our social
   media presence and connections with students. We understand the concerns that inspire those cautionary meetings and the policy that, as
   educators, we may not be social media friends with our students. Yet
   we think it is possible for it to work. In fact, if we really mean we want to
   teach students positive habits of digital citizenship, then it is essential
   that we interact with them in digital communities. The use of closed Facebook groups and searchable hashtags allows teachers and students to
   interact on social media platforms like Facebook and Twitter and still
   maintain a separation of their personal lives. Further separation can be
   achieved by the creation of classroom accounts. And there is precedent
   for these groups existing as many student-athletes, their families, and
   coaches communicate in such groups, as do other extra- and cocurricular
   school groups. However teachers and administrators choose to structure conversations, we aren't really teaching digital citizenship or information literacy if we aren't digital neighbors.

9

A Longer Unit of Study

What follows is a broad outline of the essential questions for a media literacy course that would give students guided opportunity for the creation of positive online personas, the examination of good habits of digital conduct, and the application of their digital literacy to real-world problem solving.

UNIT 1: SHOULD I SHARE THIS?

Historically, our innate need to receive and share information seems to go hand in hand with censorship. From Martin Luther's revolution made possible by the printing press to digital media distributed via the small computers we euphemistically call phones, the power of creating, curating, and distributing information is immense. Napoleon once said, "Four hostile newspapers are more to be feared than a thousand bayonets." As librarians, each year we promote banned books and websites in order to increase our students' understanding that their access to information is a privilege—while it should be a right—that they need to safeguard. Furthermore, when choosing to exercise that right, we tacitly accept responsibility for participating in a manner that advances civil discourse. The challenge of teaching cyber citizen-students to be good digital citizens is helping them to create space, a moment of reflection, between stimulus and response—teaching them to be mindful. You might remember the days of walking down the hallway at school and shoving a note through the vents in a friend's locker. And some people shoved unkind notes through locker vents. But, more often than not, the time it took to walk the halls of the school and find the target locker created that space between the stimulus that prompted the writing of an unkind message and the response of slipping it through the vents of the recipient's locker. That hallway walk created the space necessary for better angels to prevail in many cases. What makes today different is the immediacy with which a response to a stimulus can be created and disseminated. A challenge of digital citizenship education is to prompt students to be mindful, to breathe before posting, to reflect on their response before sending it, to consider whether that response is something they want to be permanently etched into their digital profile. We need to help our students to approach every digital interaction with the same caution that they might employ when they hear the buzz of a tattoo needle. Building empathy is the key to helping students hit the pause button rather than acting (or posting) on impulse. To that end, Unit 1 addresses these questions:

- What is my online persona, and how can I be sure it represents me accurately?
- What is news, and how do I know when something is true?
- What is my role curating information (consumer, producer, disseminator)?

UNIT 2: HOW CAN SOMETHING BE BOTH BIASED AND MEANINGFUL?

What is true evolves as a news story unfolds. Journalistic truth provides to information consumers the best available account of an event based on the available, verifiable facts at any given time. Even when publishing objective news stories, journalists exercise editorial judgment, balancing what their audience wants to know with what they need to know. The target audience for any publication of information is a critical element in determining the manner in which the content is portrayed and disseminated. Professional journalists are trained to remain neutral when reporting; their bylines assure information consumers of their accountability for impartiality or bias. News consumers must remember that opinions included in reporting don't always indicate bias and that commentary is a part of reporting. One important gauge of the quality of an information source or news outlet is whether that publication or agency separates objective reporting from editorial content. News consumers need to know that the content of the editorial pages does not influence the objective reporting of the news.

- The many faces of me—when may I have an opinion, and when must I refrain from bias? Which platform is for which purpose (or which face of me)?
- When I encounter new information, how do I know when the author's bias interferes with the meaning and substance?
- How can I hold my own biases loosely so they do not interfere with what I can learn and understand?

RESOURCES

American Press Institute: "Understanding Bias" and tools to manage bias: https://www.americanpressinstitute.org/journalism-essentials/bias-objectivity/understanding-bias/

"How Do I Tell When the News Is Biased? It Depends on How You See Yourself": Switched front pages—how we are framed to see and understand media:
http://www.niemanlab.org/2012/06/how-do-you-tell-when-the-news-is-biased/

"Is Glenn Greenwald the Future of News?": Interesting dialogue about the future of news reporting and the relationship between reporters and their stories:
http://www.nytimes.com/2013/10/28/opinion/a-conversation-in-lieu-of-a-column.html

Society for Professional Journalists Ethics Code:
https://www.spj.org/ethicscode.asp

"The Times Issues Social Media Guidelines for the Newsroom": *New York Times* newsroom policy for social media:
https://www.nytimes.com/2017/10/13/reader-center/social-media-guidelines.html

UNIT 3: WHY CAN'T I SEPARATE THE MEDIUM FROM THE MESSAGE?

We all have our preferred modes of communication. Frequently those preferences may vary generationally. Creators of content understand those variations. Ads play on television on certain networks at certain times of day to reach the demographic audience most likely to be watching at those times. The same principles are true of other modes of information transmission. The products and ideas sold to a 19-year-old within the video game he is playing (yes, advertisers can and do infiltrate your games) aren't the same or aren't portrayed in the same way as the products sold to his 50-year-old mother in her Facebook feed. The same principles apply to fake news or intentional misinformation and hoaxes. The creators of this type of information rely on digital manipulation of images and video and digital transmission to reach wide audiences through viral resharing. Message, audience, and medium are inextricably linked.

- How do advertisers use different media to sell the same product or message?
- How has the evolution of media changed the way in which information is created, distributed, accessed, and used?
- When deciding how to share what I have learned, how will I consider my audience? Message? Purpose? And create a product that meets all of these needs?

RESOURCES

"Breaking News Consumer's Handbook," WNYC
https://www.snopes.com/Snopes:
http://www.wnyc.org/shows/otm/handbooks

"Educator's Guide: Types of Online Fakes," Verification Handbook:
http://verificationhandbook.com/additionalmaterial/types-of-online-fakes
.php

"Fake News. It's Complicated," First Draft News:
https://firstdraftnews.com/fake-news-complicated/

"Fake or Real? How to Self-Check the News and Get the Facts," NPR):
https://www.npr.org/sections/alltechconsidered/2016/12/05/503581220/fake
-or-real-how-to-self-check-the-news-and-get-the-facts

"For the 'New Yellow Journalists,' Opportunity Comes in Clicks and Bucks,"
The Washington Post:
https://www.washingtonpost.com/national/for-the-new-yellow-journalists
-opportunity-comes-in-clicks-and-bucks/2016/11/20/d58d036c-adbf-11e6
-8b45-f8e493f06fcd_story.html?utm_term=.3e3c770c4c2b

Grasswire examines social media images in real time to expose hoaxes:
https://www.grasswire.com/
https://twitter.com/grasswire

Hoax-Slayer:
http://www.hoax-slayer.net/recent-posts-latest-information/

"How Fake News Sites Frequently Trick Big-Time Journalists," *Columbia Journalism Review*
https://www.cjr.org/analysis/how_fake_news_sites_frequently_trick_big
-time_journalists.php

"The 7 Reasons People Believe in Conspiracy Theories," Urban Legends (About
.com):
https://www.thoughtco.com/urban-legends-4132595

"7 Vital Browser Plugins for Newsgathering and Verification," First Draft News:
https://firstdraftnews.com/5-vital-browser-plugins-for-newsgathering-and
-verification-journalism-social-media/

"7 Ways to Spot and Debunk Fake News," *Newsday*
https://www.newsday.com/opinion/7-ways-to-spot-and-debunk-fake-news-1
.12695382

"13 Online Tools That Help to Verify the Authenticity of a Photo," StopFake.org:
https://www.stopfake.org/en/13-online-tools-that-help-to-verify-the-authen
ticity-of-a-photo/

TruthOrFiction:
http://www.truthorfiction.com/

"We Tracked Down a Fake-News Creator in the Suburbs. Here's What We Learned," NPR: https://www.npr.org/sections/alltechconsidered/2016/11/23/503146770/npr-finds-the-head-of-a-covert-fake-news-operation-in-the-suburbs

"What Is Fake News? How to Spot It and What You Can Do to Stop It," *The Guardian*: https://www.theguardian.com/media/2016/dec/18/what-is-fake-news-pizzagate

UNIT 4: PROBLEM-BASED LEARNING: HOW CAN I USE DIGITAL MEDIA FOR GOOD?

Digital media has transformed our relationship with information and therefore with the global community. We are instantly aware of events happening around the world, and we can hear the sounds of war and terror, as well as those of harmony and jubilation. We are moved to act by the video footage we see of natural and human-caused disasters. And we join movements for change because we see them playing out on our devices in our hands. Professional conferences even have hashtags for the people not in attendance to follow (#notataasl7)! As we equip our students with the tools and skills requisite to recognizing and not being duped by hoaxes and misinformation, we must go further and empower them to be digital leaders. The most effective way to combat purposeful, ill intentioned misinformation is by elevating and magnifying the voices engaged in informed civil discourse. Students must learn to use social media not just for interacting with friends far and wide. They must also learn to engage and organize through digital media, researchers, advocates, fund-raisers, politicians, nonprofit organizations, and other problem solvers in order address the needs of their communities.

- What issue, problem, or cause do I care about? Why?
- How can I take informed action?
- How can I contribute to a solution or remedy?
  - Design cycle
  - Presentation of plan
- Whom am I trying to reach (who is my audience)?
- How do those people most frequently access information? Why?
- What is the best media for conveying my evidence and conclusions? Consider:
  - Do I need photographs or other artist renderings?
  - Do I need data visualization?
  - Are voices, music, or other auditory files important to understanding my message?
  - Is there a need for video footage?
  - How much text do I have? Does it require hyperlinks or interactivity?

- How will my product reach my audience?
  - Will it live on a website?
  - Should I post to a video sharing forum like YouTube?
  - Should the product be delivered via e-mail?
  - Does it exist in printed form?
  - Should it be performed or delivered to a live audience?
  - Something else?
- How will the talents of my team combine to create a successful product or presentation?

REFERENCES

Casa-Todd, Jennifer. *Social LEADia: Moving Students from Digital Citizenship to Digital Leadership.* N.p.: Dave Burgess Consulting, 2017.

Jenkins, Henry, et al. *By Any Media Necessary: The New Youth Activism.* New York: New York University Press, 2016.

10

Rubrics

A note on the development and use of these rubrics:

Grades, points and percentages facilitate data collection and analysis that can be used to review and describe student progress. However, that data does not necessarily or likely invite student reflection and revision. For this reason, the rubrics included here do not include point values. By highlighting portions of the rubric that describe a student's process and product on a draft of an assignment, we try to encourage student reflection on their academic, creative, and collaborative habits of mind so that they can set goals for each new task based on their learning from previous ones.

Research Paper Rubric

	Exemplary	Accomplish	Developing	Beginning
Knowledge	Demonstrates sophisticated understanding of fundamental and higher-order thinking skills and concepts Accesses, applies, documents, and presents knowledge with fluency showing full understanding of skills and concepts	Demonstrates adequate understanding of fundamental skills and concepts and some higher-order thinking ones Accesses, applies, documents, and presents knowledge with minor flaws that do not diminish understanding of skills and concepts	Demonstrates adequate understanding of either fundamental skills or concepts, with limited ability to work with higher-order thinking skills Accesses, applies, documents, and presents knowledge with flaws that diminish understanding of skills and concepts	Demonstrates limited understanding of fundamental skills and concepts, prohibiting understanding of higher-order ones Lacks fluency in accessing, applying, documenting, and presenting knowledge
Knowledge Transfer	Independently builds on prior knowledge, synthesizing and applying new information Makes frequent, meaningful and rich cross-discipline and/or real-life connections	Builds on prior knowledge, synthesizing and applying new information, with minimal support Makes relevant cross-discipline and real-life connections	Builds on prior knowledge and ideas with support, resulting in minimal synthesis and application Attempts some cross-discipline and real-life connections that demonstrate partial understanding	Rarely builds on prior knowledge and ideas, even with support, prohibiting synthesis and application Learns primarily without cross-discipline or real-life connections
Active Inquiry	Initiates and sustains exploration of relevant and sophisticated questions Demonstrates resourcefulness in accessing productive and substantive information	Poses and considers relevant questions Accesses relevant information	Poses and considers new questions with prompting Needs direction in accessing relevant information	Seldom poses new questions Has difficulty accessing information

Critical Thinking and Problem Solving	Identifies complex problems Effectively evaluates quality and validity of information from multiple perspectives Proposes solutions that are thoroughly supported and demonstrates sophisticated understanding	Identifies problems Evaluates quality and validity of information Proposes logical solutions that are adequately supported	Identifies problems with support Evaluates information with support Proposes solutions with limited or flawed evidence	Seldom identifies problems Has difficulty evaluating information Has difficulty proposing logical solutions
Historical Thinking Persuasion, interpretation, corroboration, and contextualization	Consistently interprets evidence accurately; fairly represents people, issues and events; factual details and chronology are accurate Recognizes and explores bias and interpretation in source materials; evidence is balanced and credible Synthesizes multiple pieces of evidence to support thesis; recognizes and addresses conflicting evidence Establishes clear historical contexts and develops cause–effect relationships; recognizes and explores original meaning of sources for audience at time of source creation	Generally interprets evidence accurately; fairly represents people, issues and events but may lack completeness; factual details and chronology are accurate Recognizes bias but unable to challenge, compare, or reconcile biases Compares or contrasts sources but does not synthesize them to generate new or unique ideas Demonstrates basic understanding of chronology; may not thoroughly develop cause–effect relationships	While some evidence is accurate and portrayals are fair, inaccuracies and misrepresentations distract from meaning Bias may be recognized but is not balanced or bias is not recognized, so apparent balance is not conscious and purposeful Conflicting evidence may be recognized but not resolved or addressed Lacking meaningful context; errors in chronology	Evidence is inaccurate, irrelevant or suspect; people are ignored or misrepresented; chronology and details are inaccurate Does not recognize bias; unknowingly presents bias as fact; information is not balanced, sources lack credibility No corroborating evidence; ignores conflicting sources of evidence No historical context

(continued)

Research Paper Rubric (*continued*)

	Exemplary	Accomplish	Developing	Beginning
Presentation Organization, Fluency, Voice, Tone, Grammar, Mechanics	Demonstrates logical organization where each paragraph enlarges and deepens the meaning or central idea; organization may or may not be conventional Shows exceptional clarity and fluency, transitions work well, skillfully blends quotations Exhibits personal voice and style because the writer knows the effect language has on the audience; the personality of the writer is evident; the writer's enthusiasm and/or interest brings the topic to life; the writing is natural and compelling; the tone is appropriate and consistently controlled; the overall effect is individualistic, expressive, and engaging; includes the language specific to purpose; uses language artfully and articulately Follows appropriate style guide (e.g., MLA) Consistently applies rules of grammar, mechanics, and usage accurately Shows sophisticated sense of audience Meaningfully organizes Uses media/materials effectively	Demonstrates logical organization but lacks the sophistication of those devices used in the top category; shows clarity and fluency Transitions are obvious or generic; blends quotations Exhibits personal voice and style but lacks the sophistication of those devices used in the top category, uses language effectively Follows appropriate style guide (MLA); sometimes lacks accuracy Consistently applies most rules of grammar, mechanics, and usage; still learning Shows clear sense of audience Clearly organized Uses media/materials appropriately	Demonstrates acceptable organization; shows some clarity and fluency Transitions and blending of quotations are inconsistent or awkward False and forced voice; generic style because hasn't yet developed the strategies necessary; does not take the audience into consideration; uses language somewhat effectively Misunderstands or misapplies style guide' frequent MLA errors Lacking experience with or knowledge of rules of grammar, mechanics, and usage evidenced by frequent errors Shows some sense of audience Somewhat organized Somewhat appropriate use of media/materials	Disorganized; demonstrates a lack of clarity and fluency; writes in an unclear and choppy manner, no transitions; does not blend quotations Lacks personal voice and style Style guide? Ignores or is unaware of rules of grammar, mechanics, and usage Shows little sense of audience Uses language ineffectively Weak organization interferes with meaning Ineffective use of media/materials

Reflection (Metacognition) Rubric

	Bill and Ted's Excellent Adventure	Almost Famous	Gone with the Wind	Apocalypse Now
Sophistication of Personal Insight	Reflection includes extensive, personal responses to the issues raised in the course of study; demonstrates understanding of personal growth; thoughtful and convincing	Reflection demonstrates that the student is beginning to develop new ways of reflecting on the world and the content; thoughtful but predictable	Reflection includes some personal response to the issues/concepts raised in the course of study; reflection is a simple restatement of the content presented in class	Little or no personal response is made to the issues/concepts raised in the texts; little or no evidence of reflection
Analysis and Content Connections	Reflection incorporates information and ideas culled from a range of contexts; demonstrates social, political, historical, awareness; consistently demonstrates insight about the relevance of the content to self and society; reviews and deepens understanding of previous course content in the context of each new unit, topic, or concept addressed	Reflection incorporates a limited range of ideas and information; may be convincing but lacking sophisticated exploration; generic understanding of the relevance of the content to self and society; connects new and old content but doesn't deepen understanding of previous content in the context of new units, topics, or concepts	Reflection alludes to what student has heard in class but is limited to superficial generalizations; limited understanding of the relevance of the content to self and society; periodically connects new information with earlier content but is still unable to achieve more sophisticated understanding of either	Student makes little or no reference to what is heard in class or outside class; no understanding of the relevance of the content to self and society or earlier content
Metacognition and Self-Regulation	Works with a sense of deliberativeness; intentionally forms a vision of a product, plan of action, goal, or a destination before beginning; strives to clarify and understand directions, develops a strategy for approaching a problem and withholds immediate judgments about an idea before fully understanding it; considers	Reflects with each task but only because instructed to; may not track progress over all Usually able to articulate why an approach is (or is not) successful but doesn't see the connection to learning (unless prompted) May use past reflection for goal setting	Reflects with little depth because hasn't yet developed the strategies for doing it; does not track progress Cannot articulate what, why, or how a process was used or why a process worked or did not work	Blurts the first answer that comes to mind; starts to work without fully understanding the directions; lacks an organized plan or strategy for approaching a problem or makes immediate value judgments about an

(continued)

Reflection (Metacognition) Rubric (*continued*)

Bill and Ted's Excellent Adventure	Almost Famous	Gone with the Wind	Apocalypse Now
alternatives and consequences of several possible directions prior to taking action; decreases the need for trial and error by gathering information, reflects on an answer before giving it, listens to alternative points of view	Always recounts what was done, beginning to understand the process for doing it (how) and the rationale for using that process (why); beginning to evaluate the process to see strengths/successes and areas for improvement	May record what was done, but the reflections are simple recounting of the steps of the process; no attempt at analyzing the process is made	idea—criticizing or praising it—before fully understanding it; may take the first suggestion given or operate on the first idea that comes to mind rather than considering alternatives and consequences of several possible directions
Knows what she/he knows and doesn't know; able to plan a strategy for producing what information is needed, conscious of steps and strategies during the act of problem solving; reflects on and evaluates the productiveness of own thinking; increasingly aware of own actions and the effect of those actions on others; forms internal questions as searches for information and meaning, develops mental maps or plans of action; mentally rehearses prior to performance; monitors those plans as they are employed—being conscious of the need for midcourse correction if the plan is not meeting expectations; reflects on the plan upon completion of the implementation for the purpose of self-evaluation; and edits mental pictures for improved performance		Attempts to understand but generally resorts to trial and error because sees it as easier (even if less productive)	Makes no effort to understand own thinking; resorts to trial and error consistently; cannot (or doesn't try to) recognized gaps in knowledge in order to seek new information

Advertising Rubric

	"The Way You Do the Things You Do" The Temptations	"Knockin' on Heaven's Door" Originally Bob Dylan	"Unchained Melody" The Righteous Brothers	"What's Goin' On?" Marvin Gaye
General Appearance and Aesthetics	Strong aesthetic appeal; not cluttered, graphics enhance content; image selection is appropriate; makes you want to continue watching; enhancements enrich the viewing and learning experience and significantly contribute to conveying the content and meaning; sustained and seamless use of technical devices, and content relevant visuals establish a clear visual pattern that aids audience understanding	Multimedia elements adequately contribute to conveying the content and meaning; most graphics used appropriately to enrich the experience, although purpose may not be readily evident; purposeful use of animations and devices; main points are evident on slides and expanded through presentation; good, relevant visuals	Lacking attention to aesthetic design; graphics are random or do not enhance content; overuse of animations and technical animations/devices; too much text, needs to be condensed	Graphics interfere with or distract from content and communication of ideas; inappropriate or no use of animations, devices, images; a paper on the screen
Critical Thinking and Content Mastery	The presentation of ideas is thoughtful, insightful, clear, and focused; approaches the topic from an unusual perspective, using unique experiences or view of the world as a basis for communicating; makes interesting connections between ideas; implicit that this exploration matters Explores the complexity of the issues; in-depth analysis; confrontation and discussion of conflicting information, motivations and ideas; critical research evident;	Attempts to develop all ideas, although some ideas may be developed more thoroughly and specifically than others; the overall development reflects some depth of thought, enabling the viewer to generally understand and appreciate the ideas Analysis accurate but lacking depth of understanding; may not demonstrate clear understanding of audience motivation; may lack thoroughness in addressing purpose.	Limited by superficial generalizations; unclear or simplistic; may be simply an account of a single incident instead of articulating a purpose; therefore the viewer cannot sustain interest in the ideas More descriptive than analytic; relies on summary of information and events rather than application of information	Confusing and hard to follow; disorganized; develops no connections among ideas; statements are convoluted, and viewer is left questioning the ad itself and not the ideas presented in the ad Inadequate or inaccurate understanding of the information, events or audience; attempts at analysis or insight are confused or

(continued)

Advertising Rubric (continued)

	"The Way You Do the Things You Do" The Temptations	"Knockin' on Heaven's Door" Originally Bob Dylan	"Unchained Melody" The Righteous Brothers	"What's Goin' On?" Marvin Gaye
	interprets principles in accurate and insightful ways	Considerable evidence contributes to message development but lacks depth; assumptions cloud facts, some ideas are ambiguous.	to audience opinion; makes errors in interpreting research; ineffectively synthesizes the information	inappropriate; major errors in understanding
	Thoroughly researched; all points substantiated by evidence; no assumptions; sophisticated understanding of details, nuances and subtleties of the content		Exhibits only sketchy or insufficient evidence; may have errors; some understanding of details, nuances and subtleties of the content; most subject knowledge is literal and does not enhance message development	Almost no use of evidence; attempts are confused or inappropriate; major errors; complete misunderstanding or no effort to understand the details, nuances and subtleties of the content
	Sufficient information to make the ad worth watching; information is conveyed; content effectively achieves its intended purpose; historical information is accurate and relevant			

Multimedia Presentation Rubric

	"The Way You Do the Things You Do" The Temptations	"Knockin' on Heaven's Door" Originally Bob Dylan	"Unchained Melody" The Righteous Brothers	"What's Goin On?" Marvin Gaye
General Appearance and Aesthetics	Strong aesthetic appeal; not cluttered, graphics enhance content; image selection is appropriate; makes you want to continue interacting; enhancements enrich the viewing and learning experience and significantly contribute to conveying the content and meaning Sustained and seamless use of technical devices and content relevant visuals establish a clear visual pattern that aids audience understanding	Multimedia elements adequately contribute to conveying the content and meaning; most graphics used appropriately to enrich the experience; although purpose may not be readily evident Purposeful use of animations and devices; main points are evident and expanded through presentation; good, relevant visuals	Lacking attention to aesthetic design. Graphics are random or insufficient and do not enhance content Overuse of animations and technical animations/devices; too much text, needs to be condensed	Graphics interfere with or distract from content and communication of ideas; inappropriate or no use of animations, devices, images; an essay on the screen
Critical Thinking and Content Mastery	The presentation of ideas is thoughtful, insightful, clear, and focused; approaches the topic from an unusual perspective, using unique experiences or view of the world as a basis for communicating; makes interesting connections between ideas; it is implicit that this exploration matters Explores the complexity of the issues; in-depth analysis;	Attempts to develop all ideas; although some ideas may be developed more thoroughly and specifically than others; the overall development reflects some depth of thought, enabling the viewer to generally understand and appreciate the ideas Analysis accurate but lacking depth of understanding; may not demonstrate clear understanding	Limited by superficial generalizations; unclear or simplistic; may be simply an account of a single incident instead of articulating a purpose; therefore the viewer cannot sustain interest in the ideas More descriptive than analytic; relies on	Confusing and hard to follow; disorganized; develops no connections among ideas; statements are convoluted, and viewer is left questioning the work itself and not the ideas presented in the work Inadequate or inaccurate understanding of the

(continued)

Multimedia Presentation Rubric (continued)

	"The Way You Do the Things You Do" The Temptations	"Knockin' on Heaven's Door" Originally Bob Dylan	"Unchained Melody" The Righteous Brothers	"What's Goin On?" Marvin Gaye
	confrontation and discussion of conflicting information, motivations and ideas; critical research evident; interprets principles in accurate and insightful ways Thoroughly researched; all points substantiated by evidence; no assumptions; sophisticated understanding of details, nuances, and subtleties of the content; sufficient information to make the presentation worth reading or viewing; information is conveyed; content effectively achieves its intended purpose; historical information is accurate and relevant Makes frequent, meaningful and rich cross-discipline and/or real-life connections	of audience motivation; may lack thoroughness in addressing purpose Considerable evidence contributes to message development but lacks depth; assumptions cloud facts, some ideas are ambiguous Makes relevant cross-discipline and real-life connections	summary of information and events rather than application of information to audience opinion; makes errors in interpreting research; ineffectively synthesizes the information Exhibits only sketchy or insufficient evidence; may have errors; some understanding of details, nuances, and subtleties of the content; most subject knowledge is literal and does not enhance message development Attempts some cross-discipline and real-life connections that demonstrate partial understanding	information, events, or audience; attempts at analysis or insight are confused or inappropriate; major errors in understanding Almost no use of evidence; attempts are confused or inappropriate; major errors; complete misunderstanding or no effort to understand the details, nuances, and subtleties of the content Learns primarily without cross-discipline or real-life connections
Presentation	Shows sophisticated sense of audience; uses language artfully and articulately; meaningfully organizes; uses media/materials effectively	Shows clear sense of audience; uses language effectively; clearly organizes; uses media/materials appropriately	Shows some sense of audience; uses language somewhat effectively; somewhat organized; somewhat appropriate use of media/materials	Shows little sense of audience; uses language ineffectively; weak organization interferes with meaning; ineffective use of media/materials

Podcast Rubric

Content Delivery	Best Day of My Life	Pearly Gates	Not a Bad Thing	Wrecking Ball
	Catchy and clever introduction	Describes the topic and engages the listener as the introduction proceeds; shows clear sense of audience	Somewhat engaging (covers a well-known topic) and provides a vague purpose; shows some sense of audience	Irrelevant or inappropriate topic that minimally engages the listener. Does not include an introduction, or the purpose is unclear; shows little sense of audience
	Provides relevant information and establishes a clear purpose that engages the listener immediately; shows sophisticated sense of audience			
	Identifies speaker, as well as date podcast was produced and location of speaker	Tells most of the following: who is speaking, date of the podcast, and location of speaker	Alludes to who is speaking, date of the podcast, and location of speaker	Speaker is not identified. Omits the date the podcast was produced and location of speaker.
	Uses language artfully and articulately	Uses language is effectively	Uses language somewhat effectively	Uses language ineffectively; vocabulary is inappropriate for the audience.
	Accesses, applies, documents, and presents knowledge with fluency showing full understanding of skills and concepts	Accesses, applies, documents, and presents knowledge with minor flaws that do not diminish understanding of skills and concepts	Accesses, applies, documents, and presents knowledge with flaws that diminish understanding of skills and concepts	Lacks fluency in accessing, applying, documenting, and presenting knowledge
	Initiates and sustains exploration of relevant and sophisticated questions; demonstrates resourcefulness in accessing productive and substantive information	Poses and considers relevant questions; accesses relevant information	Poses and considers new questions with prompting; needs direction in accessing relevant information	Seldom poses new questions; has difficulty accessing information
	Keeps focus on the topic	Stays on the topic	Occasionally strays from the topic	Does not stay on topic.
	Conclusion clearly summarizes key information	Conclusion summarizes information	Conclusion vaguely summarizes key information	No conclusion is provided
	The podcast is well rehearsed and delivered smoothly; the enunciation is clear and intelligible; and there is much expression and enthusiasm in the recitation	The podcast is rehearsed and delivered smoothly, the enunciation is clear and intelligible, and there is expression and enthusiasm in the recitation	The podcast is rehearsed, the enunciation is sometimes clear and intelligible, and there is some expression and enthusiasm in the recitation	The podcast appears unrehearsed, the enunciation is muddled and not clear, and the recitation lacks expression and enthusiasm

(continued)

Podcast Rubric (continued)

	Best Day of My Life	Pearly Gates	Not a Bad Thing	Wrecking Ball
Technical Production	The volume is good for both music and voice, there is no background or other distracting noise, and there are no technical glitches; the music selected enhances the podcast, fits the mood and content of the piece, and is at a volume level that does not overpower the voice The podcast shows care and effort The quality of the production is excellent The speech is fluent, and the speed of delivery is acceptable The podcast is enhanced with high-quality and appropriate sound effects and music that make the podcast more captivating and enjoyable	The volume is good for both music and voice, there is little background or other distracting noise, and there are no technical glitches. The music selected is appropriate for the podcast, fits the mood and content of the piece, and is at a volume level that does not overpower the voice. The podcast shows care and effort. The quality of the production is good with few issues regarding quality i.e. high or low sound levels, background noise, hiss, sibilance, poor cuts and fades long periods of silence, unbalanced etc. The speech is fluent and the speed of delivery is acceptable. The podcast is enhanced with sound effects and music	The volume is fair for both music and voice; there is background and other distracting noise; and there are some technical glitches. The music selected is somewhat appropriate for the podcast, somewhat fits the mood and content of the piece, and is at a volume level that sometimes overpowers the voice or is barely audible. The podcast shows some care and effort is taken The quality of the production is acceptable with some issues regarding quality, i.e., high or low sound levels, background noise, hiss, sibilance, poor cuts and fades, long periods of silence, unbalanced, etc. The speech is fluent but has some pauses, hums, etc. The speed of delivery is acceptable Music or sound effects are of acceptable quality and for the most part appropriate	The volume is poor for both music and voice; there is considerable background and other distracting noise; and there are several technical glitches There is no music, or the music selected is not appropriate for the podcast, does not fit the mood and content of the piece, and is at a volume level that overpowers the voice or is not audible at all The podcast shows little care or effort. The quality of the production is poor, i.e., high or low sound levels, background noise, hiss, sibilance, poor cuts and fades, long periods of silence, unbalanced, etc. The speech lacks fluency, is punctuated by pauses, hums, etc.: the speed of delivery is too slow or rushed Music or sound effects are of not of an acceptable quality or are inappropriate

Teamwork			
Proactively works toward group goals Consistently and actively contributes knowledge, opinions, and skills Values the knowledge, opinions, and skills of all group members and encourages their contribution Performed all duties of assigned team role and contributed knowledge, opinions, and skills to share with the team Always did the assigned work	Contributes to group goals without prompting Contributes knowledge, opinions, and skills Values the knowledge, opinions, and skills of all group members Assisted group/partner Performed nearly all duties and contributed knowledge, opinions, and skills to share with the team Completed the assigned work	Finished own part but did not assist group/partner Works toward group goals with occasional prompting Contributes knowledge, opinions, and skills with prompting Sometimes recognizes the knowledge, opinions, and skills of all group members	Did not perform any duties of assigned team role and did not contribute knowledge, opinions, or skills to share with the team Relied on others to do the work Worked toward group goals only when prompted Rarely contributed knowledge, opinions, and skills without prompting Rarely recognizes the knowledge, opinions, and skills of all group members

Works Cited

Adams, Sarah. "Be Cool to the Pizza Dude." *This I Believe*. May 16, 2005. http://thisibelieve.org/essay/23/. https://www.npr.org/2005/05/16/4651531/be-cool-to-the-pizza-dude.

"AllSides Dictionary." *AllSides*. Accessed January 10, 2018. http://www.allsides.com/dictionary.

Atwan, Robert. *Convergences: Message, Method, Medium*. 2nd ed. New York: St. Martin's Press, 2004.

Bergstrom, Carl T., and Jevin West. "Syllabus." *Calling Bullshit: Data Reasoning in a Digital World*. University of Washington. Accessed January 10, 2018. http://callingbullshit.org/syllabus.html.

"'Boys on the Bus': 40 Years Later, Many Are Girls." Transcript. National Public Radio. April 12, 2012. http://www.npr.org/templates/transcript/transcript.php?storyId=150577036.

Bruni, Frank. "College Admissions Shocker!" *New York Times*, March 30, 2016. http://nytimes.com/2016/03/30/opinion/college-admissions-shocker.html.

Carter, Prudence L. "Poor Schools Need to Encompass More Than Instruction to Succeed." *New York Times*, September 14, 2016. http://nytimes.com/roomfordebate/2016/09/14/is-school-reform-hopeless/poor-schools-need-to-encompass-more-than-instruction-to-succeed.

"Censoring the Press." Learning Network. *New York Times*. Accessed January 10, 2018. http://static01.nyt.com/images/blogs/learning/pdf/activities/CensoringPress_NYTLN.pdf.

Colbert, Stephen. "The Word—Truthiness." *The Colbert Report* video, 2:40. October 17, 2005. http://cc.com/video-clips/63ite2/the-colbert-report-the-word---truthiness.

Colbert, Stephen. "The Word—Wikiality." *The Colbert Report* video, 4:10. July 31, 2006. http://cc.com/video-clips/z1aahs/the-colbert-report-the-word---wikiality.

"Dorothea Lange's 'Migrant Mother' Photographs in the Farm Security Administration Collection: An Overview." Compiled by Prints and Photography

Division, Library of Congress. 2004. http://www.loc.gov/rr/print/list/128 _migm.html.

Farhi, Paul. "Sean Hannity Thinks Viewers Can Tell the Difference between News and Opinion. Hold on a Moment." *Washington Post*, March 28, 2017. http:// washingtonpost.com/lifestyle/style/sean-hannity-thinks-viewers-can-tell -the-difference-between-news-and-opinion-hold-on-a-moment/2017/03/27 /eb0c5870-1307-11e7-9e4f-09aa75d3ec57_story.html.

Filucci, Sarah. "How to Spot Fake News (and Teach Kids to Be Media-Savvy)." *CommonSense Media* (blog). March 20, 2017. http://commonsensemedia.org/blog /how-to-spot-fake-news-and-teach-kids-to-be-media-savvy.

Gottfried, Jeffery, and Elisa Shearer. "News Use across Social Media Platforms 2016." *Pew Research Center: Journalism & Media.* May 26, 2016. http:// journalism.org/2016/05/26/news-use-across-social-media-platforms-2016.

Graff, Gerald, and Cathy Birkenstein. *"They Say/I Say": The Moves That Matter in Academic Writing.* 3rd ed. New York: W. W. Norton, 2014.

Haglund, David. "How Accurate Is *Argo*?" *Slate.* October 12, 2012. http://slate.com /blogs/browbeat/2012/10/12/argo_true_story_the_facts_and_fiction_behind _the_ben_affleck_movie.html.

Heimans, Jeremy. "What New Power Looks Like." TED video, 15:09. June 2014. Accessed January 3, 2017. https://www.ted.com/talks/jeremy_heimans_what _new_power_looks_like/transcript.

"Imagine This: A Super Bowl Ad for the Government." Transcript. All Things Considered. National Public Radio. February 4, 2011. Accessed January 10, 2017. http://npr.org/2011/02/04/133504071/Imagine-This-A-Super-Bowl -Ad-For-The-Government.

Kahne, Joseph, and Benjamin Bowyer. "Educating for Democracy in a Partisan Age: Confronting the Challenges of Motivated Reasoning and Misinformation." *American Educational Research Journal* 54, no. 1 (February 2017): 3–34. http:// civicsurvey.org/sites/default/files/publications/Educating_for_Democracy _in_a_Partisan_Age.pdf.

Klein, Gil. "What's Wrong with This Picture?" *Colonial Williamsburg Journal.* Winter 2001. http://history.org/foundation/journal/winter11/painting.cfm.

Knorr, Caroline. "Three Easy Ways Google, Facebook, and Twitter Help Kids Sniff out Fake News." *Salon.* Salon Media Group. May 12, 2017. Accessed January 2, 2017. https://www.salon.com/2017/05/12/three-easy-ways-google-facebook -and-twitter-help-kids-sniff-out-fake-news_partner.

Krulwich, Robert. "Krulwich Wonders: Whose Fingers Are on the Victoria's Secret Model's Shoulder?" *RadioLab.* WNYC Studios. February 1, 2012. http://radiolab .org/story/184792-krulwich-wonders-whose-fingers-are-victorias-secret -models-shoulder.

LaFrance, Adrienne. "We Fact-Checked Snapple's 'Real Facts.'" *Atlantic.* The Atlantic Monthly Group. October 11, 2013. http://theatlantic.com/technology/arc hive/2013/10/we-fact-checked-snapples-real-facts/280512.

The Learning Network. "Censoring the Press." *New York Times.* http://static01.nyt .com/images/blogs/learning/pdf/activities/CensoringPress_NYTLN.pdf. Accessed January 10, 2018.

"Lesson Plans." *Teach Argument.* http://teachargument.com/products. Accessed January 10, 2018.

Morgan, Edmund S. *The Birth of the Republic 1763–89.* Chicago: University of Chicago Press, 1977.

National Archives and Records Administration. "Document Analysis Worksheets." *Teacher Resources.* United States Government. Accessed January 10, 2018. http://www.archives.gov/education/lessons/worksheets.

New York City School Library System. "Empire State Information Fluency Continuum". New York City Department of Education. Accessed January 10, 2018. http://schools.nyc.gov/NR/rdonlyres/1A931D4E-1620-4672-ABEF-460 A273D0D5F/0/EmpireStateIFC.pdf.

On the Media. WNYC Studios. Accessed January 10, 2018. https://www.wnyc.org /shows/otm.

"The Opinion Pages: Joe Nocera." *New York Times.* http://nytimes.com/column /joe-nocera. Accessed January 10, 2018.

"The Opinion Pages: Paul Krugman." *New York Times.* http://nytimes.com/column /paul-krugman. Accessed January 10, 2018.

"Our Mission." *FactCheck.org.* Annenberg Public Policy Center. Accessed January 10, 2018. https://factcheck.org/about/our-mission.

"The PolitiFact Staff." *Politifact. Tampa Bay Times.* Accessed January 10, 2018. http://politifact.com/truth-o-meter/staff.

Porter, Eduardo. "Education Gap between Rich and Poor Is Growing Wider." *New York Times,* September 22, 2015. http://nyti.ms/2kjPphU.

Reardon, Sean F., Jane Waldfogel, and Daphna Bassok. "The Good News about Educational Inequality." *New York Times,* August 26, 2016. https://nyti.ms /2kt0KfT.

Revkin, Andy. "Tools and Techniques for Tracking How #FakeNews (or the Real Thing) Flows". August 23, 2016. http://medium.com/@revkin/to-see-how -information-flows-online-try-a-backtrack-journal-e5e65e56bf6c.

Richards, Sam. "A Radical Experiment in Empathy." TED video, 18:07. October 2012. http://ted.com/talks/sam_richards_a_radical_experiment_in_empathy.

Rosenthal, Norman E. "Using Meditation to Help Close the Achievement Gap," *New York Times,* June 2, 2016. https://well.blogs.nytimes.com/2016/06/02 /using-meditation-to-help-close-the-achievement-gap.

Rothstein, Dan, and Luz Santana. *Make Just One Change.* Cambridge, MA: Harvard Education Press, 2011.

United Nations Educational, Scientific, and Cultural Organization. "Five Laws of Media and Information Literacy." *UNESCO Communication and Information.* Accessed January 10, 2018. http://unesco.org/new/en/communication-and -information/media-development/media-literacy/five-laws-of-mil.

"Week in Politics." National Public Radio. http://npr.org/2017/05/19/529175716 /week-in-politics-fallout-continues-over-firing-of-fbi-director-comey/. Accessed January 10, 2018.

"Week in Rap." *Flocabulary.* Accessed January 10, 2018. https://www.flocabulary .com/topics/week-in-rap.

Wineburg, Sam, Sarah McGrew, Joel Breakstone, and Teresa Ortega. "Evaluating Information: The Cornerstone of Civic Online Reasoning." Stanford Digital Repository. 2016. http://purl.stanford.edu/fv751yt5934.

"Why the Achievement Gap Persists." Editorial. *New York Times,* December 8, 2006. http://nytimes.com/2006/12/08/opinion/08fri1.html.

Zinn, Howard. *A People's History of the United States.* New York: Harper Perennial Modern Classics, 2005.

Index

About the Authors

JACQUELYN WHITING is library media specialist at Wilton High School in Wilton, Connecticut. She is a Certified Google Innovator with a concentration in media literacy and digital citizenship. She is the winner of the 2017 Connecticut Association of School Librarians' Carlton W. H. Erickson Award for an auspicious beginning in media services and was the 2016 recipient of the Connection Region 9 Teacher of the Year award. She has taught in high schools for 24 years.

MICHELLE LUHTALA is Library Department Chair at New Canaan High School in New Canaan, Connecticut. She facilitates an online learning community for nearly 12,000 library and educational technology professionals at edWeb .net/emergingtech, where she has hosted over 85 webinars since 2010. She is an adjunct instructor in the Information and Library Science Program at Southern Connecticut State University and is also a contributing author to Libraries Unlimited's *Growing Schools: Librarians as Professional Developers*. Michelle was named a Mover & Shaker by Library Journal in 2015 and the American Association of School Librarians distinguished her as Curriculum Champion in 2017.